THE DUAS BOOK
from
QURAN & HADITH

"Allah has revealed the best announcement in
the form of a Book, consistent with itself, repeating
(itst eaching in various aspects): the skins of those who fear their Lord
tremble thereat;"

FULFILMENT OF RELIGIOUS NEEDS

A. الم ۝ اللهُ لَا إِلَهَ إِلَّا هُوَ الْحَىُّ الْقَيُّومُ ۝

Alif Laam Meem. Allah!
There is none worthy of worship but He,
The Ever-Living, The Eternal.

Al Imran 1,2

Significance: According to some *Hadith*. The *Ismul-A'zam* is contained in this verse. It is most effective if read continually in times of calamity.

B. لَا إِلَهَ إِلَّا أَنْتَ سُبْحَانَكَ إِنِّى كُنْتُ مِنَ الظَّالِمِينَ

None is worthy of worship besides You.
You are Pure (and) surely, I am from among the transgressors.

Al Ambiya 87

Significance: The *Ismul-A'zam* is according to other traditions contained in the above verse. A person will profit tremendously if he recites it for any legitimate purpose.

C. هُوَ اللهُ الَّذِى لَا إِلَهَ إِلَّا هُوَ عَلِمُ الْغَيْبِ وَالشَّهَدَةِ

$$\text{هُوَ الرَّحْمَٰنُ الرَّحِيمُ ۝}$$

Allah is He besides whom there is none worthy of worship.
He is the Knower of both secret and open.
He is Most Kind, Most Merciful.

Al Hashr 22

Significance: The *Ismul-A'zam* is, according to some, concealed in the above verse. Anyone who recites it seven times in the morning, an angel will be appointed to seek pardon on his behalf till the evening. If he happens to die on that day, he will die as a *martyr*. 'And if he reads it seven times in the evening, the angels will seek pardon for him till the morning. If he happens to die during the night, he will die as a *martyr*.

DEATH IN THE STATE OF IMAN

$$\text{رَبَّنَا لَا تُزِغْ قُلُوبَنَا بَعْدَ إِذْ هَدَيْتَنَا وَهَبْ}$$

$$\text{لَنَا مِنْ لَدُنْكَ رَحْمَةً إِنَّكَ أَنْتَ الْوَهَّابُ ۝}$$

Our Lord! Let not our hearts deviate after You have guided us.
And (instead) grant us Your special mercy,
for You are the Granter of bounties without limits.

Al Imran 8

Significance: Anyone who recites this *Du'a* after each *Salaah*, he shall die in the state of *Iman* — *Insha Allah*.

PARDON FROM ALLAH ﷻ

$$\text{رَبَّنَا ظَلَمْنَا أَنْفُسَنَا وَإِنْ لَّمْ تَغْفِرْ لَنَا وَتَرْحَمْنَا}$$

7

$$\text{لَنَكُوَنَنَّ مِنَ الْخُسِرِيَنَ ﴿٢٣﴾}$$

Our Lord! We have wronged our souls:
If You do not forgive us and bestow upon us Your mercy,
then we shall certainly be from amongst the losers.

Al A'raf 23

Significance: Anyone who recites this *Du'a* once after every Fardh *Salaah*, Allah ﷻ will grant him pardon - *Insha-Allah*. This is the *Du'a* of Adam عليه السلام after he was transferred on to the earth.

SHAFA'AH (INTERCESSION OF RASULULLAH ﷺ)

$$\text{لَقَدْ جَاءَكُمْ رَسُوَلٌ مِّنْ اَنْفُسِكُمْ عَزِيَزٌ عَلَيَهِ}$$

$$\text{مَا عَنِتُّمْ حَرِيَصٌ عَلَيَكُمْ بِالْمُؤْمِنِيَنَ رَءُوَفٌ رَّحِيَمٌ ﴿١٢٨﴾}$$

$$\text{فَإِنْ تَوَلَّوَا فَقُلْ حَسْبِيَ اللهُ لَآ إِلَهَ إِلَّا هُوَ}$$

$$\text{عَلَيَهِ تَوَكَّلْتُ وَهُوَ رَبُّ الْعَرْشِ الْعَظِيَمِ ﴿١٢٩﴾}$$

Surely, an Apostle from amongst you has come unto you:
Your harms grieve him: he is ardently anxious over you:
to the Believers he is mot kind and merciful. But if they turn away,
say: 'Allah suffices me: There is none worthy of worship but He:
upon Him is my trust - He is Lord of the Great Throne.'

At Tawbah 128,129

Significance: Whoever recites these verses once after every *Salaah*, he will attain the intercession of Rasulullah ﷺ on the *Day of Judgement* - *Insha-Allah*. Moreover, it is very effective in removing any harm.

STEADFASTNESS OF THE HEART

$$\text{فَاسْتَقِمْ كَمَآ أُمِرْتَ وَمَنْ تَابَ مَعَكَ}$$

Be firm (upon the Right Path) just as You had been commanded
and those who had repented with You, (had been commanded).

Hud 112

Significance: For steadfastness of the heart, recite 11 times after every *Salaah*.

CREATING *NOOR* IN THE HEART

A. SURAH AL KAHF

Significance: Whoever recites *Surah Al Kahf* once every Friday, his heart will remain filled with *noor* till the following Friday. Whoever recites the first 10 verses of this *Surah* every day, he will be safe-guarded against the *fitnah* of *Dajjal*.

REMOVING SUSPICION AND DOUBT

My Lord! I seek your protection from the prompting
of the Devils; and my Lord! I seek your protection
from them approaching me.

Al Muminun 97,98

Significance: The excessive recitation of the above verses removes all suspicion and doubt.

PIETY IN THE FAMILY

رَبَّنَا هَبْ لَنَا مِنْ اَزْوَاجِنَا وَذُرِّيّٰتِنَا قُرَّةَ اَعْيُنٍ
وَّاجْعَلْنَا لِلْمُتَّقِيْنَ اِمَامًا ۝

***Our Lord, let our wives and offspring be a means of
the coolness of our eyes and make us the leaders
of the righteous people.***

Al Furqan 74

Significance: Anyone desirous of righteous children and a righteous
wife should recite the above verse once after each *Salaah*.

PROTECTION FROM THE FIRE OF HELL

حٰمٓ ۝ تَنْزِيْلُ الْكِتٰبِ مِنَ اللهِ الْعَزِيْزِ الْعَلِيْمِ ۝

حٰمٓ ۝ تَنْزِيْلٌ مِّنَ الرَّحْمٰنِ الرَّحِيْمِ ۝

حٰمٓ ۝ عٓسٓقٓ ۝

حٰمٓ ۝ وَالْكِتٰبِ الْمُبِيْنِ ۝

حٰمٓ ۝ وَالْكِتٰبِ الْمُبِيْنِ ۝

اِنَّا اَنْزَلْنٰهُ فِيْ لَيْلَةٍ مُّبٰرَكَةٍ اِنَّا كُنَّا مُنْذِرِيْنَ ۝

Ha. Mim. *This Heavenly Book is sent down from Allah,*
the Almighty, the All-Knowing-
Ha. Mim. This Quran has been sent down from Allah,
the Most-Kind, the Ever-Merciful.
Ha. Mim. Ain. Sin. Qaf.
Ha. Mim. By the Book luminous!
Ha. Mim. By the Luminous Book that makes plain
the Truth- Surely We have sent it down during
a blessed night-truly it is for Us to give
timely warning (against evil).
Ha. Mim. This Heavenly Book has been sent down from Allah,
the Almighty, the All-Wise.
Ha. Mim. This Heavenly Book is sent down from Allah,
the Almighty, the All-Wise.

Significance: Anyone who recites the above seven *Ha Mims* constantly, the door of Hell-fire will always remain closed for him, but a person should rather try to recite as much of the Qur'an as possible.

NOOR ON THE FACE

Truly, it is He who is Beneficent, Merciful.

At Tur 28

Significance: Anyone who recites the above verse 11 times, his face will shine brightly on the *Day of Qiyamah ... Insha-Allah.*

11

SAFETY FROM PUNISHMENT IN THE GRAVE

Significance: Anyone who recites *Surah Al-Mulk* daily will be safeguarded against the punishment of the grave.

AWAKENING IN THE NIGHT

A. وَإِذْ جَعَلْنَا الْبَيْتَ مَثَابَةً لِّلنَّاسِ وَأَمْنًا ۖ وَاتَّخِذُوا مِنْ مَّقَامِ اِبْرٰهِمَ مُصَلًّى ۖ وَعَهِدْنَآ اِلٰى اِبْرٰهِمَ وَاِسْمٰعِيْلَ اَنْ طَهِّرَا بَيْتِيَ لِلطَّآئِفِيْنَ وَالْعٰكِفِيْنَ وَالرُّكَّعِ السُّجُوْدِ ۞

And remember the time when We made The House
a place of worship for the people and a place of safety.
And take the Maqam Ibrahim as a place of performing Salaah.
And We decreed to Ibrahim and Isma'il that they should purify
My House for those who observe Tawaaf of it and those
who observe Ruku and those who observe Sajdah (in prayers)
Al Baqarah 125

Significance: It was found written by a certain sage, that anyone who recites the above verse before retiring to bed, he will be able to get up at any time he desires.

B. اِنَّ فِيْ خَلْقِ السَّمٰوٰتِ وَالْأَرْضِ وَاخْتِلَافِ الَّيْلِ وَالنَّهَارِ لَأَيٰتٍ لِّأُولِى الْاَلْبٰبِ ۞ الَّذِيْنَ يَذْكُرُوْنَ اللّٰهَ قِيٰمًا وَّقُعُوْدًا وَّعَلٰى جُنُوْبِهِمْ وَيَتَفَكَّرُوْنَ فِيْ خَلْقِ السَّمٰوٰتِ وَالْاَرْضِ ۚ

رَبَّنَا مَا خَلَقْتَ هٰذَا بِطِلًا ۚ سُبْحٰنَكَ فَقِنَا عَذَابَ النَّارِ ۝

رَبَّنَآ اِنَّكَ مَنْ تُدْخِلِ النَّارَ فَقَدْ اَخْزَيْتَهٗ ۗ وَمَا لِلظّٰلِمِيْنَ

مِنْ اَنْصَارٍ ۝ رَبَّنَآ اِنَّنَا سَمِعْنَا مُنَادِيًا يُّنَادِىْ لِلْاِيْمٰنِ اَنْ

اٰمِنُوْا بِرَبِّكُمْ فَاٰمَنَّا ۖ رَبَّنَا فَاغْفِرْ لَنَا ذُنُوْبَنَا وَكَفِّرْ عَنَّا

سَيِّاٰتِنَا وَتَوَفَّنَا مَعَ الْاَبْرَارِ ۝ رَبَّنَا وَ اٰتِنَا مَا وَعَدْتَّنَا عَلٰى

رُسُلِكَ وَلَا تُخْزِنَا يَوْمَ الْقِيٰمَةِ ۗ اِنَّكَ لَا تُخْلِفُ الْمِيْعَادَ ۝

Verily in the creation of the heavens and the earth,
and in the alternation of night and day
there are (mighty) signs for men of understanding-
Those men of understanding who remember Allah standing
and sitting and lying on their sides, and keep reflecting on the
wonders of the creation of the heavens and the earth (and admit
saying): "Our Lord! You have not created all this (Universe) in vain.
Glory be to You! Save us Lord!
from the torment of the Blazing Fire.
"Our Lord! whomsoever You cause to enter Hell,
him You have surely disgraced, and for the wrongdoers
there shall be no helpers.
"Our Lord! we have heard a proclaimer calling to Faith (saying):
'Believe in your Lord;' so we have come to believe.
Our Lord! forgive us our sins, and wipe off our misdeeds from us
and cause us (in all grace) to die with the righteous.
"Our Lord! grant us that which You have promised to us through

Your Apostles and disgrace us not on the Day of Reckoning.
Surely You never fail in your Promise."

Al Imran 190,194

Significance: Anyone who recites the first 5 verses of the last Ruku of *Surah Al-Imran* before going to bed, his *Iman* will remain intact and he will be able to wake up at any time he desires without any assistance whatsoever.

TO SIMPLIFY THE MEMORIZING OF THE QUR'AN

Significance: Recite *Surah Muddath-thir*, then make *Du'a. Insha-Allah* memorising the *Qur'an* will become easy.

MAINTAINING CORRECT BELIEFS

Significance: Excessive recitation of *Surah Al-Ikhlaas* will enable a person to adopt and maintain correct beliefs and safeguard himself against *shirk*.

CORRECTING ONE'S BELIEFS

Significance: Recite *Surah Al-Ikhaas* morning and evening. It is very effective in safeguarding one's *Iman* and beliefs.

PLEASURE OF ALLAH ﷻ

اَلْعَفُوُّ

The Forgiver of Sins

Significance: To have one's sins atoned and to gain the pleasure of the Almighty, recite the above name of Allah ﷻ excessively.

REMOVING OF A CALAMITY

$$\text{حَسْبُنَا اللّٰهُ وَنِعْمَ الْوَكِيْلُ ﴿١٧٣﴾}$$

Allah suffices for us and He is the Best Disposer of affairs.

Al Imran 173

Significance: Continuous recitation of the above *verse* is very effective in removing all difficulties and calamities.

ASSURED ACCEPTANCE OF DUA

٨. اِنَّ فِىْ خَلْقِ السَّمٰوٰتِ وَالْاَرْضِ وَاخْتِلَافِ الَّيْلِ وَالنَّهَارِ

لَاٰيٰتٍ لِّاُولِى الْاَلْبَابِ ﴿١٩٠﴾ الَّذِيْنَ يَذْكُرُوْنَ اللّٰهَ قِيَامًا وَّقُعُوْدًا

وَّعَلٰى جُنُوْبِهِمْ وَيَتَفَكَّرُوْنَ فِىْ خَلْقِ السَّمٰوٰتِ وَالْاَرْضِ

رَبَّنَا مَا خَلَقْتَ هٰذَا بَاطِلًا ۚ سُبْحٰنَكَ فَقِنَا عَذَابَ النَّارِ ﴿١٩١﴾

رَبَّنَا اِنَّكَ مَنْ تُدْخِلِ النَّارَ فَقَدْ اَخْزَيْتَهٗ ۭ وَمَا لِلظّٰلِمِيْنَ

مِنْ اَنْصَارٍ ﴿١٩٢﴾ رَبَّنَا اِنَّنَا سَمِعْنَا مُنَادِيًا يُّنَادِىْ لِلْاِيْمَانِ اَنْ

اٰمِنُوْا بِرَبِّكُمْ فَاٰمَنَّا ۖ رَبَّنَا فَاغْفِرْ لَنَا ذُنُوْبَنَا وَكَفِّرْ عَنَّا

سَيِّاٰتِنَا وَتَوَفَّنَا مَعَ الْاَبْرَارِ ﴿١٩٣﴾ رَبَّنَا وَ اٰتِنَا مَا وَعَدْتَّنَا عَلٰى

رُسُلِكَ وَلَا تُخْزِنَا يَوْمَ الْقِيٰمَةِ ؕ اِنَّكَ لَا تُخْلِفُ الْمِيْعَادَ ۝

For Translation See Awaking at Night on page 14

Significance: Rasulullah ﷺ used to recite the above *verses* after *Tahajjud Salaah*. The fact that Rasulullah ﷺ used to recite them after *Tahajjud* is sufficient proof as to the assured acceptance of the *Du'a* that appear in them. Any *Du'a* made after their recital will also be accepted by Allah ﷻ — *Insha-Allah*.

B. فَقُلْتُ اسْتَغْفِرُوْا رَبَّكُمْ ؕ اِنَّهٗ كَانَ غَفَّارًا ۝ يُّرْسِلِ السَّمَآءَ عَلَيْكُمْ مِّدْرَارًا ۝ وَّيُمْدِدْكُمْ بِاَمْوَالٍ وَّبَنِيْنَ وَيَجْعَلْ لَّكُمْ جَنّٰتٍ وَّيَجْعَلْ لَّكُمْ اَنْهٰرًا ۝

And I said: Ask forgiveness from your Lord
for He is Oft-Forgiving
He will send rain to you in abundance,
He will give you increase in wealth and sons
and bestow on you gardens and bestow on you rivers.

Nuh 10,12

Significance: *Du'a* are certainly accepted after *Istighfar* as understood from the above.

C. اَللّٰهُ لَآ اِلٰهَ اِلَّا هُوَ ۚ اَلْحَىُّ الْقَيُّوْمُ ۚ لَا تَاْخُذُهٗ سِنَةٌ وَّلَا نَوْمٌ ؕ لَهٗ مَا فِى السَّمٰوٰتِ وَمَا فِى الْاَرْضِ ؕ مَنْ ذَا الَّذِىْ يَشْفَعُ عِنْدَهٗ

اِلَّا بِاِذْنِهٖ ۚ يَعْلَمُ مَا بَيْنَ اَيْدِيْهِمْ وَمَا خَلْفَهُمْ ۚ وَلَا يُحِيْطُوْنَ بِشَىْءٍ مِّنْ عِلْمِهٖٓ اِلَّا بِمَا شَآءَ ۚ وَسِعَ كُرْسِيُّهُ السَّمٰوٰتِ وَالْاَرْضَ ۚ وَلَا يَـُٔوْدُهٗ حِفْظُهُمَا ۚ وَهُوَ الْعَلِيُّ الْعَظِيْمُ ۞

Allah, none is worthy of worship except He,
the Hayyul Qayyoom (the ever-living, the One who
sustains and protects all that exists).
Neither slumber nor sleep overtakes Him.
To Him belongs whatever is in the heavens and earth.
Who is there that can intercede before Him except
by His permission? He knows what happens to them
before them and behind them.
And they will never encompass anything of
His knowledge except that which He wills.
His throne extends over the heavens and earth.
And He feels no fatigue in guarding them.
And He is Most High, Most Great.

Al Baqarah 255

Significance: Recite *Aayatul-Kursi* 70 times after Asr *Salaah* on Friday. Sit in seclusion while doing this. A special and marvelous feeling will be experienced in the heart. Any *Du'a* made after this, will be assuredly accepted by Allah ﷻ — *Insha-Allah*.

D.

اَلْمُجِيْبُ

The One who Responds.

Significance: For the assured acceptance of *Du'a* call upon Allah ﷻ by His above attribute numerous times while making *Du'a*.

FULFILMENT OF ANY NEED

But if they away, say: Allah suffices me.
None is worthy of worship but He.
On Him is my trust and He is the
Lord of the Supreme Throne.

At Tawbah 129

Significance: Abu Darda ﷺ relates that any person who recites the above *ayah* 100 times, all his worldly needs and his needs pertaining to the Hereafter will be fulfilled.

IMPROVING THE MEMORY

My Lord! Expand for me my bosom.
Ease my task for me.
Remove the knot from my speech so that
they may understand what I say.

Ta-Ha 25,28

Significance: For strengthening the memory and progressing in knowledge recite the above verses everyday after Fardh *Salaah*.

REMOVING FEAR AND GRIEF

Significance: The recitation of *Surah Nooh* is very effective in removing grief and fear. Also *Surah Yasin* is most effective in removing all types of fear — especially for one's life. It is reported from *Ibnul-Kalbi* that a certain person's life had been threatened. He reported the matter to an *alim* who advised him to recite *Surah Yasin* every time he leaves his home. He did exactly as he was told with the result that every time he came before his enemy, the latter failed to see him.

ACQUIRING A SON

رَبِّ هَبْ لِيْ مِنْ لَّدُنْكَ ذُرِّيَّةً طَيِّبَةً ۚ

إِنَّكَ سَمِيْعُ الدُّعَآءِ ﴿٣٨﴾

O My Lord! Grant me from Yourself a progeny that is pure:
for You are the Granter of prayers.

Al Imran 38

Significance: By the excessive recitation of the above verse, a person will acquire a virtuous and righteous son. — *Insha Allah*.

VIRTUOUS CHILDREN

رَبِّ لَا تَذَرْنِيْ فَرْدًا وَّأَنْتَ خَيْرُ الْوٰرِثِيْنَ ﴿٨٩﴾

O my Lord! Do not leave me without offspring.
Surely, You are the best of inheritors.

Al Ambiya 89

Significance: Recite the above *ayah* three times after every *Salaah*. Good and righteous children will be granted — *Insha Allah*.

STERILITY

اَلْبَارِئُ الْمُصَوِّرُ

The Shaper out of naught, The Fashioner.

Significance: If a barren woman fasts for seven days and after breaking her fast with water, (she should eat food thereafter) reads the above Name of Allah ﷻ 21 times then she will soon conceive — *Insha Allah*.

MISCARRIAGE

A. اَللّٰهُ يَعْلَمُ مَا تَحْمِلُ كُلُّ اُنْثٰى وَمَا تَغِيضُ الْاَرْحَامُ

وَمَا تَزْدَادُ ۔ وَكُلُّ شَيْءٍ عِنْدَهٗ بِمِقْدَارٍ ۞

Allah knowns that which every female bears and that which the wombs absorb and that which they grow. And everything with Him is measured.

Ar Ra'd 8

Significance: If there is fear of miscarriage the above verse should be recited.

LABOUR PAINS

اَوَلَمْ يَرَ الَّذِيْنَ كَفَرُوْۤا اَنَّ السَّمٰوٰتِ وَالْاَرْضَ كَانَتَا رَتْقًا

فَفَتَقْنٰهُمَا ۗ وَجَعَلْنَا مِنَ الْمَآءِ كُلَّ شَىْءٍ حَىٍّ ۗ اَفَلَا يُؤْمِنُوْنَ ۩

Have not those who disbelieve known that the
heavens and the earth were of one piece,
then We parted them, and We made every living thing of water?
Will they not then believe?

Al Ambiya 30

Significance: When a woman is in the throes of labour, the above *verse* should be recited by someone (female or mahram male) and then *blown* on the stomach or back of the woman.

PROTECTING CHILDREN AGAINST INFANTILE DISEASES

اِنِّيْ تَوَكَّلْتُ عَلَى اللهِ رَبِّيْ وَرَبِّكُمْ ۗ مَا مِنْ دَآبَّةٍ اِلَّا هُوَ اٰخِذٌ

بِنَاصِيَتِهَا ۗ اِنَّ رَبِّيْ عَلٰى صِرٰطٍ مُّسْتَقِيْمٍ ۩

Lo! have put my trust in Allah, My Lord and your Lord.
There is not an animal but He (Allah) grasps it by its forelock!
Lo! My Lord is on the Straight Path.

Hud 56

Significance: To protect a child from such sicknesses which normally afflict children, the above *ayah* should be recited and blown on the child.

HEALTHY UPBRINGING OF CHILDREN

الَّذِىْٓ اَحْسَنَ كُلَّ شَىْءٍ خَلَقَهٗ وَبَدَاَ خَلْقَ الْاِنْسٰنِ مِنْ

طِينٍ ۞ ثُمَّ جَعَلَ نَسْلَهُ مِن سُلَٰلَةٍ مِّن مَّآءٍ مَّهِينٍ ۞

ثُمَّ سَوَّىٰهُ وَنَفَخَ فِيهِ مِن رُّوحِهِ وَجَعَلَ لَكُمُ السَّمْعَ

وَالْأَبْصَٰرَ وَالْأَفْئِدَةَ ۚ قَلِيلًا مَّا تَشْكُرُونَ ۞

He Who made everything par excellence which He created,
and He began the creation of man from clay.
Then He created his progeny from an extract of mean water.
Then He set him aright in form and feature and breathed into
him of His Spirit, and He gave you ears, eyes and hearts.
But you give little thanks (for these gifts).

As Sajdah 7

Significance: The above verses should be recited and du'a should be made.

FOR ABUNDANCE IN RIZQ

A.

اللَّهُ لَطِيفٌ بِعِبَادِهِ يَرْزُقُ مَن يَشَآءُ ۖ

وَهُوَ الْقَوِيُّ الْعَزِيزُ ۞

Allah is gracious unto His slaves —
He provides for whom He wills.
And He is the Strong, the Mighty.

As Shura 19

Significance: For increment in one's *rizq*, recite the above *ayah* excessively after each *Salaah*.

22

B. وَمَنْ يَّتَوَكَّلْ عَلَى اللّٰهِ فَهُوَ حَسْبُهٗ ۚ إِنَّ اللّٰهَ بٰلِغُ أَمْرِهٖ ۚ

قَدْ جَعَلَ اللّٰهُ لِكُلِّ شَىْءٍ قَدْرًا ۝

And whoever puts his trust in Allah, He will suffice him.
Lo! Allah brings His commands to pass.
Allah has set a measure for all things.

At Talaq 3

Significance: Excessive recitation of the above *ayah* is very effective in removing poverty. If it is recited for any purpose, it will be realised — *Insha Allah.*

C. Surah Al Qalam

Significance: Recitation of *Surah Al-Qalam* in *Salaah* removes poverty.

D. Surah Al Qari'ah

Significance: Excessive recitation of *Surah Al-Qari'ah* is very effective in increasing one's *rizq.*

REPAYMENT OF DEBTS

قُلِ اللّٰهُمَّ مٰلِكَ الْمُلْكِ تُؤْتِى الْمُلْكَ مَنْ تَشَآءُ وَتَنْزِعُ

الْمُلْكَ مِمَّنْ تَشَآءُ وَتُعِزُّ مَنْ تَشَآءُ وَتُذِلُّ مَنْ تَشَآءُ ۚ بِيَدِكَ

الْخَيْرُ ۚ إِنَّكَ عَلٰى كُلِّ شَىْءٍ قَدِيْرٌ ۝

23

Say: O Allah! Master of the sovereignty!
You give sovereignty to whomever You desire,
and withdraw sovereignty from whomever You desire.
You exalt whomever You desire and debase whomever You desire.
In Your hand is goodness.
Truly, You possess power over everything.

Al Imran 26

Significance: Recite the above verse seven times after Fajr and seven times after Maghrib. *Insha Allah*, Allah ﷻ will make means for debts to be settled.

TO PLEASE SOMEONE ENDOWED WITH POWER

A.

كَمْ اٰتَيْنٰهُمْ مِّنْ اٰيَةٍ بَيِّنَةٍ ۫ وَمَنْ يُّبَدِّلْ نِعْمَةَ اللهِ مِنْ بَعْدِمَا جَآءَتْهُ فَاِنَّ اللهَ شَدِيْدُ الْعِقَابِ ﴿٢١١﴾

How many a clear revelation we bestowed upon them.
He who after the grace of Allah after it been granted to him,
Allah will punish him. Lo! Allah is severe in punishment.

Al Baqarah 211

Significance: Recite the following *verse* thrice and then blow on yourself. After doing this go before the person endowed with power (such as a chief, judge etc.) *Insha Allah* he will display much sympathy and leniency.

سُبْحٰنَ اللهِ وَتَعٰلٰى عَمَّا يُشْرِكُوْنَ ﴿﴾ وَرَبُّكَ يَعْلَمُ مَا تُكِنُّ صُدُوْرُهُمْ وَمَا يُعْلِنُوْنَ ﴿﴾ وَهُوَ اللهُ لَآ اِلٰهَ اِلَّا هُوَ ۫

$$\text{لَهُ الْحَمْدُ فِى الْأُوْلَىٰ وَالْأَخِرَةِ ، وَلَهُ الْحُكْمُ وَاِلَيْهِ تُرْجَعُوْنَ}$$

*Glorified be Allah and exalted above
all they associate (wtih Him).
And Your Lord know what their breasts
conceal and what they publish.
And He is Allah. There is no God save Him.
For Him is all praise in the former and latter (state).
For Him is command and unto Him you will be returned.*

Al Qasas 68,70

Significance: The above *ayaat* should be recited seven times when there is fear that one's opponent will give false evidence before a judge provoking him to carry out judgement wrongfully. After reciting them seven times, the following *verse* should be recited thrice before appearing in front of the judge. *Insha Allah* the reciter will be safeguarded from all forms of evil.

TO HALT AN OPPRESSOR FROM OPPRESSING

A.

$$\text{فَسَتَذْكُرُوْنَ مَآ أَقُوْلُ لَكُمْ ، وَأُفَوِّضُ}$$

$$\text{أَمْرِىٓ إِلَى اللهِ ، اِنَّ اللهَ بَصِيْرٌ بِالْعِبَادِ}$$

*And you will remember what I say unto you.
I confide my cause unto Allah.
Lo! Allah is ever watchful over his slaves.*

Al Mumin 44

Significance: Reciting the above ayah in the presence of the oppressor will safeguard the reciter from his oppression.

DISOBEDIENT CHILDREN

وَأَصْلِحْ لِيْ فِيْ ذُرِّيَّتِيْ ۚ إِنِّيْ تُبْتُ اِلَيْكَ وَاِنِّيْ مِنَ الْمُسْلِمِيْنَ ۝

And (O Allah), be gracious towards me in
the matter of my off-spring.
And surely, I have returned to You in repentance,
and surely, I am of those who surrender (to You).

Al Ahqaf 15

Significance: Anyone whose children are disobedient should recite the above *Du'a* after every *Salaah*. *Insha Allah* they will soon become obedient. But have in mind one's children when saying the word *Dhurriyyati*.

FOR INSUBORDINATION AND DISOBEDIENCE

اِنِّيْ تَوَكَّلْتُ عَلَى اللهِ رَبِّيْ وَرَبِّكُمْ ۚ مَا مِنْ دَآبَّةٍ اِلَّا هُوَ

اٰخِذٌ بِنَاصِيَتِهَا ۚ اِنَّ رَبِّيْ عَلٰى صِرَاطٍ مُّسْتَقِيْمٍ ۝

Lo! I have put my trust in Allah
who is my Lord and your Lord.
There is no animal but He grasp it by its forelock.
Verily my Lord is on the straight path.

Hud 56

Significance: If a person is guilty of insubordination, his/her forelock should be grasped and the above *ayah* be recited 3 times. Thereafter he/she should be "blown" on. By doing this, *Insha Allah*, he/she will become obedient, as in accordance to *Shariah*.

PROTECTION AGAINST EVIL MEN AND JINN

A. اَللّٰهُ لَآ اِلٰهَ اِلَّا هُوَ ۚ اَلْحَيُّ الْقَيُّوْمُ ۚ لَا تَاْخُذُهٗ سِنَةٌ وَّلَا نَوْمٌ ۗ

لَهٗ مَا فِى السَّمٰوٰتِ وَمَا فِى الْاَرْضِ ۗ مَنْ ذَا الَّذِىْ يَشْفَعُ عِنْدَهٗٓ

اِلَّا بِاِذْنِهٖ ۗ يَعْلَمُ مَا بَيْنَ اَيْدِيْهِمْ وَمَا خَلْفَهُمْ ۚ وَلَا يُحِيْطُوْنَ

بِشَىْءٍ مِّنْ عِلْمِهٖٓ اِلَّا بِمَا شَآءَ ۚ وَسِعَ كُرْسِيُّهُ السَّمٰوٰتِ

وَالْاَرْضَ ۚ وَلَا يَئُوْدُهٗ حِفْظُهُمَا ۚ وَهُوَ الْعَلِىُّ الْعَظِيْمُ ﴿٢٥٥﴾

Allah, none is worthy of worship except He,
the Hayyul Qayyoom (the ever-living, the One who
sustains and protects all that exists).
Neither slumber nor sleep overtakes Him.
To Him belongs whatever is in the heavens and earth.
Who is there that can intercede before Him except by His permission?
He knows what happens to them before them and behind them.
And they will never encompass anything of
His knowledge except that which He wills.
His throne extends over the heavens and earth.
And He feels no fatigue in guarding them.
And He is Most High, Most Great.

Al Baqarah 255

Significance: Recitation of the *ayatul Kursi* once after every *Salaah* will cause Allah ﷻ to protect the reciter against the mischief of evil men and jinn. In fact, according to one *Hadith*, the *Shaytan* acknowledged his inability to harm anyone who recites *Aayatul Kursi*.

B. Surah Al-Falaq And Surah An-Nas

Significance: The last 2 Surah of the *Holy Qur'an*. To be recited for protection against sicknesses, sorcery, etc. Reciting them before going to bed will afford the reciter security against all calamities.

C. Surah Al-Ikhlas

Significance: Help through the constant recital of *Suratul Ikhlaas,* the 3rd last Surah of the *Holy Qur'an should be sought for any calamity.*

REMOVING FEAR

And Allah is the best of Protectors and He is the Most Merciful of all who show Mercy.

Yusuf 64

Significance: One who is terrified of his enemy or fears the approach of any calamity should recite the above verse excessively. *Insha Allah* his fears will disappear and any possible calamity will be averted.

TO REMOVE FEAR AND FRIGHT

وَإِذَا قَرَأْتَ الْقُرْاٰنَ جَعَلْنَا بَيْنَكَ وَبَيْنَ الَّذِيْنَ لَا يُؤْمِنُوْنَ بِالْاٰخِرَةِ حِجَابًا مَّسْتُوْرًا ۞ وَّجَعَلْنَا عَلٰى قُلُوْبِهِمْ اَكِنَّةً اَنْ

28

يَّفْقَهُوهُ وَفِيٓ اٰذَانِهِمْ وَقْرًا ۗ وَاِذَا ذَكَرْتَ رَبَّكَ فِی
الْقُرْاٰنِ وَحْدَهٗ وَلَّوْا عَلٰى اَدْبَارِهِمْ نُفُوْرًا ۞

And (O My Apostle!) when you recite the Quran,
We set up (to intervene) between you and those
who believe not in the Hereafter a hidden
veil invisible to the eye And We put coverings on their
hearts that they may not understand it,
and (cause) a heaviness in their ears.
And when you mention your Lord alone in the Quran,
they flee away turning on their back in aversion (from the Truth)
Bani Israil 45,46

Significance: The above verses should be recited and blown on any person who is frightened, shocked or terrified. These verses are very effective in removing horrifying thoughts as well.

SECURITY AGAINST ALL HARMS

A.   اَللّٰهُ رَبُّنَا وَرَبُّكُمْ ۗ لَنَآ اَعْمَالُنَا وَلَكُمْ اَعْمَالُكُمْ ۗ
لَاحُجَّةَ بَيْنَنَا وَبَيْنَكُمْ ۗ اَللّٰهُ يَجْمَعُ بَيْنَنَا ۚ

Allah is our Lord and your Lord.
For us is our works and for you is your works.
There are no arguments between us and you.
Allah will bring us together.

Ash Shura 15

Significance: When one fears any injury from any person or animal,

29

the above verse should be recited and "blown" in the direction of such a person or animal. *Insha Allah*, the person doing this will be protected against any injury.

B. قُلْ لَّنْ يُّصِيبَنَآ اِلَّا مَا كَتَبَ اللّٰهُ لَنَا ۚ هُوَ مَوْلٰنَا ۚ

وَعَلَى اللّٰهِ فَلْيَتَوَكَّلِ الْمُؤْمِنُوْنَ ۝

Say: "Nothing shall ever happen to us except what Allah has ordained for us. He is our Maula (Lord, Helper and Protector)." And in Allah let the believers put their trust.

At-Tauba 51

وَاِنْ يَّمْسَسْكَ اللّٰهُ بِضُرٍّ فَلَا كَاشِفَ لَهٗ اِلَّا هُوَ ۚ

وَاِنْ يُّرِدْكَ بِخَيْرٍ فَلَا رَآدَّ لِفَضْلِهٖ ؕ يُصِيْبُ بِهٖ

مَنْ يَّشَآءُ مِنْ عِبَادِهٖ ؕ وَهُوَ الْغَفُوْرُ الرَّحِيْمُ ۝

And if Allah touches you with hurt, there is none who can remove it but He, and if He intends any good for you, there is none who can repel His Favour which He causes it to reach whomsoever of His slaves He wills. And He is the Oft-Forgiving, the Most Merciful.

Yunus 107

وَمَا مِنْ دَآبَّةٍ فِى الْاَرْضِ اِلَّا عَلَى اللّٰهِ رِزْقُهَا وَيَعْلَمُ

مُسْتَقَرَّهَا وَمُسْتَوْدَعَهَا ؕ كُلٌّ فِيْ كِتٰبٍ مُّبِيْنٍ ۝

*And no moving (living) creature is there on earth
but its provision is due from Allah.
And He knows its dwelling place and its deposit
(in the uterus, grave). All is in a Clear Book
(Al-Lauh Al-Mahfuz - the Book of Decrees with Allah).*

Hud 6

اِنِّيْ تَوَكَّلْتُ عَلَى اللهِ رَبِّيْ وَرَبِّكُمْ ۚ مَا مِنْ دَآبَّةٍ اِلَّا
هُوَ اٰخِذٌۢ بِنَاصِيَتِهَا ۚ اِنَّ رَبِّيْ عَلٰى صِرَاطٍ مُّسْتَقِيْمٍ ۝

*"I put my trust in Allah, my Lord and your Lord!
There is not a moving (living) creature but He has grasp of its forelock.
Verily, my Lord is on the Straight Path (the truth).*

Hud 56

وَكَاَيِّنْ مِّنْ دَآبَّةٍ لَّا تَحْمِلُ رِزْقَهَا ۖ اللهُ يَرْزُقُهَا
وَاِيَّاكُمْ ۚ وَهُوَ السَّمِيْعُ الْعَلِيْمُ ۝

*And so many a moving (living) creature carries
not its own provision! Allah provides for it and for you.
And He is the All-Hearer, the All-Knower.*

Al-'Ankabut 60

مَا يَفْتَحِ اللهُ لِلنَّاسِ مِنْ رَّحْمَةٍ فَلَا مُمْسِكَ لَهَا ۚ وَمَا يُمْسِكْ
فَلَا مُرْسِلَ لَهٗ مِنْۢ بَعْدِهٖ ۚ وَهُوَ الْعَزِيْزُ الْحَكِيْمُ ۝

*Whatever of mercy (i.e. of good),
Allah may grant to mankind, none can withhold it;*

and whatever He may withhol, none can grant it thereafter.
And He is the All-Mighty, the All-Wise.

Fatir 2

وَلَئِنْ سَاَلْتَهُمْ مَّنْ خَلَقَ السَّمٰوٰتِ وَالْاَرْضَ لَيَقُوْلُنَّ اللّٰهُ ﮐ

قُلْ اَفَرَءَيْتُمْ مَّا تَدْعُوْنَ مِنْ دُوْنِ اللّٰهِ اِنْ اَرَادَنِيَ اللّٰهُ بِضُرٍّ هَلْ

هُنَّ كٰشِفٰتُ ضُرِّهٖٓ اَوْ اَرَادَنِيْ بِرَحْمَةٍ هَلْ هُنَّ مُمْسِكٰتُ

رَحْمَتِهٖ ﮐ قُلْ حَسْبِيَ اللّٰهُ ﮐ عَلَيْهِ يَتَوَكَّلُ الْمُتَوَكِّلُوْنَ ۩

And verily, if you ask them:
"Who created the heavens and the earth?"
Surely, they will say: "Allah (has created them)."
Say: "Tell me them, the things that you invoke besides Allah -
if Allah intended some harm for me,
could they remove His harm?
Or is He (Allah) intended some mercy for me,
could they withhold His Mercy? Say:
"Sufficient for me is Allah; in Him those
who trust (i.e. believers) must put their trust."

Az-Zumar 38

Significance: Ka'ab bin Ahbar ﷺ is reported to have said that any person who recites the following seven verses everyday will have no reason to fear any type of harm, whatsoever.

C. Surah Yasin

Significance: It is reported from Ibnul-Kalbi R.A. That a man whose life had been threatened consulted an *Alim* who advised him to recite *Surah Yasin* prior to leaving his home. He did just as he was told. The result was that his enemy failed to even notice him.

CURING SOMEONE UNDER THE INFLUENCE OF EVIL

A.

اَفَحَسِبْتُمْ اَنَّمَا خَلَقْنٰكُمْ عَبَثًا وَّاَنَّكُمْ اِلَيْنَا لَا تُرْجَعُوْنَ ۝ فَتَعٰلَى اللهُ الْمَلِكُ الْحَقُّ ۚ لَاۤ اِلٰهَ اِلَّا هُوَ ۚ رَبُّ الْعَرْشِ الْكَرِيْمِ ۝ وَمَنْ يَّدْعُ مَعَ اللهِ اِلٰهًا اٰخَرَ ۙ لَا بُرْهٰنَ لَهٗ بِهٖ ۙ فَاِنَّمَا حِسَابُهٗ عِنْدَ رَبِّهٖ ؕ اِنَّهٗ لَا يُفْلِحُ الْكٰفِرُوْنَ ۝ وَقُلْ رَّبِّ اغْفِرْ وَارْحَمْ وَاَنْتَ خَيْرُ الرّٰحِمِيْنَ ۝

Do you think We have created you in jest
and that you would not be brought back to
us (for accountability)?
Hence, exalted be Allah, The True King.
None is worthy of worship besides He,
The Lord of The Throne of Honour.

Al Mu'minun 115,118

Significance: Anyone under the influence of an evil spirit — to cure him, any person should recite the above *ayaat* thrice and "blow" in a glass of water and sprinkle such water on the patient's face. Alternatively, they should be recited thrice next to his ears. Relief will be noticed instantaneously. *Insha Allah*

B. Surah Al-Fatihah, Ayatul Kursi and the beginning 5 verses of Surah Jinn.

Significance: For someone under the influence of evil spirits, recite *Surah Al-Fatihah, Ayatul Kursi* and the beginning 5 verses of *Surah Jinn*. Then blow on clean water and sprinkle it on the afflicted person's face. If the house is also suspected of any influence, the same water could be sprinkled all over the house.

TO DRIVE OUT JINN FROM A HOUSE

Significance: It is reported from Ibnu Qutaibah R.A. that a certain trader went to Basrah to do some buying and selling of dates. On his arrival in Basrah, he began inquiring for a decent accommodation but couldn't find one. After much seeking he came across a vacant house filled with spider webs. On inquiring from the people the reason for its emptiness he was told that a Jinn is believed to be occupying the house. When he approached the landlord, the latter tried to dissuade him by saying; "Why do you want to jeopardise your life? A powerful Jinn lives there! Whoever stayed there hasn't come out alive!" The trader insisted by saying; "Allah ﷻ is my helper! Please, I must have the house!"

However, the landlord had no choice but to concede to his request. From here the story is taken up by the trader. He says; "I occupied the house. Late in the night my eyes suddenly opened and I saw a dark human form approaching me, it's eyes bloodshot — as if bright flames were leaping from them. I immediately began reciting *Aayatul Kursi*. Every sentence I recited was recited by the Jinn (in an attempt to counter attack)... until I reached

$$\text{وَلَا يَئُودُهُ حِفْظُهُمَا ۚ وَهُوَ الْعَلِيُّ الْعَظِيمُ}$$

This last sentence he could not utter. I began uttering this sentence repeatedly until I saw the form disappearing. No trace of it seemed to have ever existed. I spent the rest of the night in total comfort. In the morning I scrutinised the place where the Jinn was seen... only to find its remains in the form of a small heap of ashes. Then, from nowhere a voice was heard saying; "You have burnt a poweful Jinn to ashes"! I asked; "What caused him to burn"? The voice replied; The *verse*:

$$\text{وَلَا يَئُودُهُ حِفْظُهُمَا ۚ وَهُوَ الْعَلِيُّ الْعَظِيمُ}$$

Their preserving never makes Him weary.
He is The Sublime, The Great.

IMAM AWZA'I R.A. AND THE EVIL JINN

$$\text{اَعُوْذُ بِاللهِ مِنَ الشَّيْطَانِ الرَّجِيْمِ}$$

I seek Allah's refuge from the devil accursed.

Significance: Imam Awza'i R.A. is reported to have said that once an evil Jinn suddenly confronted him, frightening him tremendously. He immediately recited the above ayah. The Jinn escaped, crying: "You have sought refuge from The Great! You have sought refuge from The Great!"

TO OVERPOWER ONE'S OPPONENT IN DEBATE

$$\text{يَاَيُّهَا النَّاسُ قَدْ جَآءَكُمْ بُرْهٰنٌ مِّنْ رَّبِّكُمْ}$$

$$\text{وَاَنْزَلْنَآ اِلَيْكُمْ نُوْرًا مُّبِيْنًا ۞ فَاَمَّا الَّذِيْنَ اٰمَنُوْا}$$

$$\text{بِاللهِ وَاعْتَصَمُوا بِهِ فَسَيُدْخِلُهُمْ فِي رَحْمَةٍ مِّنْهُ وَفَضْلٍ}$$

$$\text{وَيَهْدِيهِمْ اِلَيْهِ صِرْطًا مُّسْتَقِيمًا ۩}$$

O mankind! there assuredly has come to you a
clear proof from your Lord and We have sent down to
you a light manifest that guides you to the straight path.
Verily those who believe in Allah, and hold fast to His Rope,
very soon Allah shall cause them to enter His Mercy and Grace
and shall guide them to a straight path towards Himself.

An Nisa 174,175

Significance: To overcome an enemy in an argument one should recite the above verse.

TO OVERCOME A FOE IN ANY CONTEST OR BATTLE

A. Suratul-feel

Significance: Recitation of Suratul-feel will ensure victory for its reciters when fighting the enemy.

B. Ayatul Kursi

Significance: If Ayatul Kursi is recited before a battle, victory is a certainty, Insha Allah.

C. $$\text{سَيُهْزَمُ الْجَمْعُ وَيُوَلُّونَ الدُّبُرَ ۩}$$

The hosts will be defeated and
they will turn their backs and flee.

Al Qamar 45

Significance: Reciting the above ayah and blowing on soil, then throwing such soil in the direction of the enemy will ensure defeat of the enemy.

D.

وَمَا رَمَيْتَ اِذْ رَمَيْتَ وَلٰكِنَّ اللّٰهَ رَمٰى ۚ وَلِيُبْلِیَ

الْمُؤْمِنِیْنَ مِنْهُ بَلَآءً حَسَنًا ۚ اِنَّ اللّٰهَ سَمِیْعٌ عَلِیْمٌ ۞

اِذَازُلْزِلَتِ الْاَرْضُ زِلْزَالَهَا ۞ وَاَخْرَجَتِ الْاَرْضُ اَثْقَالَهَا ۞

وَقَالَ الْاِنْسٰنُ مَا لَهَا ۞ یَوْمَئِذٍ تُحَدِّثُ اَخْبَارَهَا ۞

بِاَنَّ رَبَّكَ اَوْحٰى لَهَا ۞ یَوْمَئِذٍ یَّصْدُرُ النَّاسُ اَشْتَاتًاه

O My Apostle! the dust that you did throw,
it was not you who threw it at them when you threw,
but Allah threw in order to bestow a
favour upon the Believers,
a goodly favour from His Presence.
Verily Allah is the All-Hearing, the All-Knowing.
When the earth is shaken to its utmost shaking -
And the earth throws up her burdens -
And man says (distressed): "What has happened to it?"
On that Day it shall narrate all its news -
For your Lord has (so) commanded it.
On that Day people will return towards their Lord,

Significance: Ibnul Kalbi reports that a very reliable person once told him about Muslims of a certain town besieged by the kuffar. A pious person amongst the Muslims recited the above verses and 'blew' on a handful of soil and had the soil scattered in the camping grounds of the enemy. The result was that the enemy began fighting amongst themselves and dispersed.

BARAKAH IN PRODUCE, LIVESTOCK, ETC.

اَللّٰهُ الَّذِىْ خَلَقَ السَّمٰوٰتِ وَالْاَرْضَ وَاَنْزَلَ مِنَ السَّمَآءِ مَآءً فَاَخْرَجَ بِهٖ مِنَ الثَّمَرٰتِ رِزْقًا لَّكُمْ ۚ وَسَخَّرَ لَكُمُ الْفُلْكَ لِتَجْرِىَ فِى الْبَحْرِ بِاَمْرِهٖ ۚ وَسَخَّرَ لَكُمُ الْاَنْهٰرَ ۞ وَسَخَّرَ لَكُمُ الشَّمْسَ وَالْقَمَرَ دَآئِبَيْنِ ۚ وَسَخَّرَ لَكُمُ الَّيْلَ وَالنَّهَارَ ۞ وَاٰتٰىكُمْ مِّنْ كُلِّ مَا سَاَلْتُمُوْهُ ۖ وَاِنْ تَعُدُّوْا نِعْمَتَ اللّٰهِ لَا تُحْصُوْهَا ۖ اِنَّ الْاِنْسٰنَ لَظَلُوْمٌ كَفَّارٌ ۞

*Allah is He Who has created the heavens and the earth
and sends down water (rain) from the sky,
and thereby brought forth fruits as provision for you;
and He has made the ships to be of service to you,
that they may sail through the sea by His Command;
and He has made rivers (also) to be of service to you.
And He has made the sun and the moon,
both constantly pursuing their courses,
to be of service to you;*

and He has made the night and the day, to be of service
to you. And He gave you of all that you asked for,
and if you count the Blessings of Allah,
never will you be able to count them.
Verily! Man is indeed an extreme
wrong-doer, a disbeliever.

Ibrahim 32,34

Significance: If recited once in the morning, once in the evening and once when going to bed, Allah ﷻ will put barakah in his crops, livestock etc. if recited before undertaking a journey Allah ﷻ will protect him and his belongings from all calamities.

BARAKAH IN BUSINESS, FARMING, HOME, ETC.

A.

بِسْمِ اللهِ الرَّحْمٰنِ الرَّحِيْمِ ۞

الٓمّٓرٰ ۚ تِلْكَ اٰيٰتُ الْكِتٰبِ ۗ وَالَّذِىٓ اُنْزِلَ اِلَيْكَ

مِنْ رَّبِّكَ الْحَقُّ وَلٰكِنَّ اَكْثَرَ النَّاسِ لَا يُؤْمِنُوْنَ ۞ اَللّٰهُ

الَّذِىْ رَفَعَ السَّمٰوٰتِ بِغَيْرِ عَمَدٍ تَرَوْنَهَا ثُمَّ اسْتَوٰى عَلَى

الْعَرْشِ وَسَخَّرَ الشَّمْسَ وَالْقَمَرَ ۗ كُلٌّ يَّجْرِىْ لِاَجَلٍ مُّسَمًّى ۗ

يُدَبِّرُ الْاَمْرَ يُفَصِّلُ الْاٰيٰتِ لَعَلَّكُمْ بِلِقَآءِ رَبِّكُمْ تُوْقِنُوْنَ ۞

وَهُوَ الَّذِىْ مَدَّ الْاَرْضَ وَجَعَلَ فِيْهَا رَوَاسِىَ وَاَنْهٰرًا ۗ وَمِنْ

كُلِّ الثَّمَرٰتِ جَعَلَ فِيهَا زَوْجَيْنِ اثْنَيْنِ يُغْشِى الَّيْلَ النَّهَارَ

اِنَّ فِيْ ذٰلِكَ لَاٰيٰتٍ لِّقَوْمٍ يَّتَفَكَّرُوْنَ ۝

In the name of Allah, Most Beneficent, Most Merciful.
Alif- Lam- Mim- Ra.
These are the Verses of the Divine Book.
And that which has been sent down to you from
your Lord is the Truth, but most of the people believe not
(because of their wrong-headedness).
Allah it is (the Mighty and the Wise) Who has raised
the heavens without pillars (as) you see them,
then He settled (Himself) on the Throne of Power,
and made the sun and the moon
subservient to His command.
Each one running its course to an appointed term.
He plans every affair, and explains clearly His Signs that haply
you maybe certain of the Meeting with your Lord.
And He it is Who has spread the earth, and
set therein firm mountains and rivers.
And fruits of every kind He has made therein in pairs,
two and two. He covers the day with the night.
Verily in all these are Signs of His Might
for a people who reflect.

Ar Ra'ad 1,3

Significance: For progress and barakah in one's business, recite these verses.

TO DRIVE AWAY PESTS

وَقَالَ الَّذِيْنَ كَفَرُوْا لِرُسُلِهِمْ لَنُخْرِجَنَّكُمْ مِّنْ   A.

اَرْضِنَآ اَوْ لَتَعُوْدُنَّ فِیْ مِلَّتِنَا ۖ فَاَوْحٰۤى اِلَیْهِمْ رَبُّهُمْ لَنُهْلِكَنَّ الظّٰلِمِیْنَ ۙ ﴿١٣﴾ وَلَنُسْكِنَنَّكُمُ الْاَرْضَ مِنْ بَعْدِهِمْ ۖ ذٰلِكَ لِمَنْ خَافَ مَقَامِیْ وَخَافَ وَعِیْدِ ﴿١٤﴾ وَاسْتَفْتَحُوْا وَخَابَ كُلُّ جَبَّارٍ عَنِیْدٍ ﴿١٥﴾ مِّنْ وَّرَآئِهٖ جَهَنَّمُ وَیُسْقٰى مِنْ مَّآءٍ صَدِیْدٍ ﴿١٦﴾ یَّتَجَرَّعُهٗ وَلَا یَكَادُ یُسِیْغُهٗ وَیَاْتِیْهِ الْمَوْتُ مِنْ كُلِّ مَكَانٍ وَّمَا هُوَ بِمَیِّتٍ ۖ وَمِنْ وَّرَآئِهٖ عَذَابٌ غَلِیْظٌ ﴿١٧﴾

And the infidels said to their Apostles:
"We will surely drive you out of our country or
you will have to come back to our religion."
So their Lord revealed to them: "(Fear not) We will certainly
destroy these wrongdoers- "And We shall certainly
settle you in their country after (destroying) them.
This (promise of success) is for him who fears the time
when he shall before Me and who fears My Warning."
And the Apostles begged for success of the Truth
(which was granted) and every obstinate rejector of Truth
was disappointed- After this (disappointment) is Hell and
he will be made to drink blood and water of oozing pus -
Which he will drink little by little with difficulty,
and will not be able to swallow it down his throat and

death will come to him from every side
but (in spite of it) he will not die.
And before him will be another dreadful torment.

Ibrahim 13,17

Significance: If crops are being destroyed by pests such as mice, worms, locust etc. then the above verses should be recited.

B. Surah Al-Tatfif

Significance: To drive out white ants from any grain and legumes such as rice, lentils beans etc. *Surah Al-Tatfif* (30th Juz) should be recited and "blown" on such foodstuff. They will disappear in a short period — *Insha-Allah*.

FOR BARAKAH AND PROGRESS IN BUSINESS

A. اِنَّ اللّٰهَ اشْتَرٰى مِنَ الْمُؤْمِنِيْنَ اَنْفُسَهُمْ وَاَمْوَالَهُمْ

بِاَنَّ لَهُمُ الْجَنَّةَ ۚ يُقْتِلُوْنَ فِىْ سَبِيْلِ اللّٰهِ فَيَقْتُلُوْنَ

وَيُقْتَلُوْنَ ۖ وَعْدًا عَلَيْهِ حَقًّا فِى التَّوْرٰىةِ وَالْاِنْجِيْلِ

وَالْقُرْاٰنِ ۚ وَمَنْ اَوْفٰى بِعَهْدِهٖ مِنَ اللّٰهِ فَاسْتَبْشِرُوْا

بِبَيْعِكُمُ الَّذِىْ بَايَعْتُمْ بِهٖ ۚ وَذٰلِكَ هُوَ الْفَوْزُ الْعَظِيْمُ ۝

Certainly Allah has purchased of the Muslims their lives and their wealth that for them in return is the Garden - the fight in the Way of Allah; so they slay and are slain.

Allah has given a solemn promise binding thereon in the Torah,
and the Gospel and the Qur'an (all the three Books).
And who is more faithful to his promise than Allah?
Rejoice, therefore, (O Believers!) in the bargain
that you have struck with Allah.
And that is indeed the supreme achievement.

At Tawbah 111

Significance: Recite the above verse for barakah and protection.

FOR PROGRESS AND PROTECTION IN BUSINESS

Significance: If *Ayatul-Kursi* is recited and "blown" on one's merchandise the following benefits will be reaped:

a. the merchandise will prove beneficial for its owner;
b. one will make good progress;
c. one will be protected from the mischief and evil promoting of Shaytan;
d. a poor person will become wealthy;
e. sustenance (rizq) will be acquired from strange and unknown sources.

If recited on entering the house and when going to bed:

a. no thieves will enter such a house;
b. the reader will not drown, burn or die due to an accident;
c. he will enjoy good health.

TO KEEP JUSTICE

اِنَّ اللهَ يَأْمُرُ بِالْعَدْلِ وَالْاِحْسَانِ وَإِيْتَآئِ ذِى الْقُرْبٰى

43

وَيَنْهٰى عَنِ الْفَحْشَآءِ وَالْمُنْكَرِ وَالْبَغْىِ

يَعِظُكُمْ لَعَلَّكُمْ تَذَكَّرُونَ ۝

**INNAL-LĀHA YA'MURU BIL `ADLI WAL
IḤSĀNI WA ĪTĀ'I DHIL QURBĀ WA YANHĀ `ANIL
FAḤSHĀ'I WAL-MUNKARI WAL-BAGHYI.
YA`IẒUKUM LA`ALLAKUM TADHAKKARŪN.**

*Allah enjoins adl (justice and worshipping none
but Allah alone) and ihsaan (to be patient in
performing your duties to Allah,
totally for Allah's sake and in accordance with sunnah)
and giving help to kith and kin
(i.e. to give them financial assistance,
visiting them, caring for them)
and He forbids you from fahshaa
(sins, evil deeds, illicit sex, disobedience to parents, lies, etc.)
and from munkar (all that is prohibited by the shari'ah)
and from baghya (oppression of all kinds).
He admonishes you so you may take heed.*

Significance: Abdullah bin Umar ﷺ narrated that once Umar ﷺ asked the people: "Who will tell me which verse in the Holy *Qur'an* is the greatest? And which verse will spur people to be just and fair? And which verse is most effective in instilling fear into the hearts of people? And which verse is most effective in building the hopes of people?" No one answered. Abdullah bin Mas'ud ﷺ finally responded by saying that he heard Rasulullah ﷺ saying on the mimbar that the greatest verse of the Holy *Qur'an* is *Ayatul Kursi*; and the above verse most effective in urging people to be just .

FOR LESSENING ONE'S BURDEN

اَلْـٰنَ خَفَّفَ اللهُ عَنْكُمْ وَعَلِمَ اَنَّ فِيْكُمْ ضَعْفًا ۚ A.

فَاِنْ يَّكُنْ مِّنْكُمْ مِّائَةٌ صَابِرَةٌ يَّغْلِبُوْا مِائَتَيْنِ ۚ وَاِنْ يَّكُنْ

مِّنْكُمْ اَلْفٌ يَّغْلِبُوْٓا اَلْفَيْنِ بِاِذْنِ اللهِ ۚ وَاللهُ مَعَ الصّٰبِرِيْنَ ﴿٦٦﴾

Now has Allah lightened Your burden for
He knows that there is weakness in you.
So if there be of you, a hundred steadfast, they shall
overcome two hundred and if there be of you a thousand
they shall overcome two thousand by the permission of Allah.
And Allah is with the steadfast.

Al Anfal 66

Significance: A person doing hard, menial work or carrying burdens on his back or doing any work that demands physical or mental exertion — if he is desirous of lessening his burden and simplifying his task — he should recite the above verse once after every *Salaah* for one week. He should start on any Friday after Asr *Salaah* and continue till the following Friday after *Jumu'ah Salaah*. *Insha Allah*, all his tasks will become easy.

WHEN ENTERING A TOWN

رَّبِّ اَنْزِلْنِيْ مُنْزَلًا مُّبَارَكًا وَّاَنْتَ خَيْرُ الْمُنْزِلِيْنَ ﴿٢٩﴾

O My Lord cause me to land at a blessed place for
You are the best of all who bring to land.

Al Mu'minun 29

Significance: Recite the above verse on entering any town, city or village. One's stay in such a place will be a pleasant one. *Insha Allah*

WHEN BOARDING ANY MEANS OF CONVEYANCE/ TRANSPORT

سُبْحٰنَ الَّذِىْ سَخَّرَ لَنَا هٰذَا وَمَا كُنَّا لَهٗ مُقْرِنِيْنَ ۟

*Glorified be He who has subdued these for us and
we were not capable of subduing them.*

Az Zukhruf 13

Significance: If the above verse is recited before boarding a vehicle, train, aircraft, ship etc. one will be protected from all forms of calamities. Insha Allah.

PROTECTION OF A VESSEL

A. بِسْمِ اللهِ مَجْرٖىٰهَا وَمُرْسٰىهَا ۚ اِنَّ رَبِّىْ لَغَفُوْرٌ رَّحِيْمٌ ۟

*In the Name of Allah be its course and its mooring.
Lo! My Lord is Most Forgiving, Ever Merciful.*

Hud 41

Significance: The above *ayah* should be recited before embarking a ship or boat. The ship and all its occupants will be safeguarded against all calamities. *Insha Allah.*

B. وَقَالَ ارْكَبُوْا فِيْهَا بِسْمِ اللهِ مَجْرٖىٰهَا وَمُرْسٰىهَآ ۚ

اِنَّ رَبِّىْ لَغَفُوْرٌ رَّحِيْمٌ ۟

*And he said: Embark therein. With the Name of Allah, be its course
and it's mooring. Lo! my Lord is Most Forgiving, Ever Merciful.*

Hud 41

Significance: This verse should also be recited before embarking the
vessel.

C. Surah Luqman

Significance: *Surah Luqman* (Juz 21). If recited before embarking a
vessel, a person will be safeguarded against drowning. *Insha Allah.*

WHEN THE SEAS ARE ROUGH

A. اَلَمۡ تَرَ اَنَّ الۡفُلۡكَ تَجۡرِىۡ فِى الۡبَحۡرِ بِنِعۡمَتِ اللّٰهِ لِيُرِيَكُمۡ

مِّنۡ اٰيٰتِهٖ ۚ اِنَّ فِىۡ ذٰلِكَ لَاٰيٰتٍ لِّكُلِّ صَبَّارٍ شَكُوۡرٍ ۩

*Have you not seen how the ships glide on the sea by
Allah's grace that He may show you of His wonders!
Lo! indeed, therein are signs for every steadfast, grateful (soul).*

Luqman 31

Significance: When the seas become rough and there is fear of
disaster, the above *ayah* should be recited. *Insha Allah* the seas will
become calm.

FOR RETURNING HOME SAFE AND SOUND

A.   اَلۡعَلِىُّ

The High

Significance: If a wayfarer (musafir) keeps a written copy of above name of Allah ﷻ he will return to his people in a short period of time. *Insha Allah* — Moreover, if he is needy, Allah will grant him abundant wealth.

B.

اَلْأَوَّلُ

The First

Significance: If a *musafir* reads above name of Allah ﷻ 1000 times every Friday, he will return to his people safely, *Insha Allah*.

FEVER

A.

اِنَّ الَّذِيْنَ اتَّقَوْا اِذَا مَسَّهُمْ طَٰٓئِفٌ مِّنَ الشَّيْطٰنِ تَذَكَّرُوْا فَاِذَا هُمْ مُّبْصِرُوْنَ ۝

***Surely those who ward off evil when a glamour from
the devil troubles them, they remember Allah and behold;
they are people of insight.***

Al A'raf 201

Significance: The above could be recited and 'blown' on a person who has a fever due to heat. Insha Allah he will soon be cured through the *barakah* of the words of Allah.

B.

قُلْنَا يٰنَارُ كُوْنِيْ بَرْدًا وَّسَلٰمًا عَلٰى اِبْرٰهِيْمَ ۝

We said: "O Fire! Become cool and peaceful for Ibrahim!"

Al Ambiya 69

Significance: The above should be recited near a sick person. Insha Allah, the fever will subside.

48

FOR ANY SICKNESS

A.

وَيَشْفِ صُدُورَ قَوْمٍ مُّؤْمِنِينَ ۞

And He will cure the breast of people who believe.

At Tauba 14

وَشِفَآءٌ لِّمَا فِى الصُّدُورِ ۚ

*And (the Qur'an) is a cure for ailments
which prevail in the hearts.*

Yunus 57

يَخْرُجُ مِنْ بُطُونِهَا شَرَابٌ مُّخْتَلِفٌ اَلْوَانُهُ فِيهِ شِفَآءٌ لِّلنَّاسِ ۗ

*There comes forth from their (the bees) bellies a drink (honey)
diverse of colours, wherein is healing for mankind.*

An Nahl 69

وَنُنَزِّلُ مِنَ الْقُرْاٰنِ مَا هُوَ شِفَآءٌ وَّرَحْمَةٌ لِّلْمُؤْمِنِينَ ۙ

*And we reveal of the Qur'an that which is a source of
healing and a source of mercy for the Believers.*

Bani Israil 82

وَاِذَا مَرِضْتُ فَهُوَ يَشْفِينِ ۞

And when I am sick, then He heals me.

Ash Shu'araa 80

قُلْ هُوَ لِلَّذِينَ اٰمَنُوْا هُدًى وَّشِفَآءٌ

Say unto them (O Muhammad!):

For those who believe, it (the Qur'an) is a guidance and a healing.
Fussilat 44

Significance: The above verses should be recited. *Insha Allah* he will be cured even if the sickness is of a serious nature.

B. وَنُنَزِّلُ مِنَ الْقُرْاٰنِ مَا هُوَ شِفَآءٌ وَّرَحْمَةٌ لِّلْمُؤْمِنِيْنَ ۙ

And we reveal of the Qur'an that which is a source of healing and a source of mercy for the Believers.
Bani Israil 82

Significance: The above *ayah* should be read and *blown* on the patient.

TO REMOVE PAIN

Significance: To relieve a patient of any pain, *Surah Yasin* should be read.

TO CURE INSOMNIA

Significance: To enable a patient to get a good sleep, *Surah Mujadalah (Juz 28)* should be recited next to the patient.

MORE PRESCRIPTIONS FOR ALL TYPES OF AILMENTS

A. اَلسَّلَامُ

The Giver of Peace

Significance: Stand by the head side of a patient and lifting the hands as in *Du'a*, say the above Name of Allah ﷻ 39 times in such a manner that the patient hears it. *Insha Allah*, he will soon be cured.

B.

اَلْعَظِيْمُ

The Great

Significance: Saying the above name of Allah ﷻ excessively will remove any sickness.

C.

اَلْحَيُّ

The Ever-Living

Significance: The above Beautiful Name of Allah ﷻ should either be recited excessively or it should be written on paper with saffron and after washing it, the water should be consumed.

D.

اَلْغَنِيُّ

The Independent

Significance: The above Name of Allah ﷻ to be recited excessively at the time of any calamity or sickness. Recovery should be expected in a short time. *Insha Allah.*

FOR MELANCHOLY AND DEPRESSION

A.

وَلِيَرْبِطَ عَلٰى قُلُوْبِكُمْ وَيُثَبِّتَ بِهِ الْاَقْدَامَ ۝

To make strong you hearts and to
keep your feet firm thereby.

Al Anfal 17

B.

اَلَّذِيْنَ اٰمَنُوْا وَتَطْمَئِنُّ قُلُوْبُهُمْ بِذِكْرِ اللّٰهِ ۫ اَلَا بِذِكْرِ

$$\text{اللهِ تَطْمَئِنُّ الْقُلُوبُ ﴿٢٨﴾}$$

Who have believed and whose hearts are at ease
in the remembrance of Allah.
Verily in the remembrance of Allah do hearts find rest.

Ar Rad 28

Significance: The above *ayaat* is very effective for removing melancholy and depression.

PALPITATION OF THE HEART

$$\text{اَفَغَيْرَ دِيْنِ اللهِ يَبْغُوْنَ وَلَهٗ اَسْلَمَ مَنْ فِى السَّمٰوٰتِ}$$

$$\text{وَالْاَرْضِ طَوْعًا وَّكَرْهًا وَّاِلَيْهِ يُرْجَعُوْنَ ﴿٨٣﴾ قُلْ اٰمَنَّا}$$

$$\text{بِاللهِ وَمَاۤ اُنْزِلَ عَلَيْنَا وَمَاۤ اُنْزِلَ عَلٰۤى اِبْرٰهِيْمَ وَاِسْمٰعِيْلَ}$$

$$\text{وَاِسْحٰقَ وَيَعْقُوْبَ وَالْاَسْبَاطِ وَمَاۤ اُوْتِيَ مُوْسٰى وَعِيْسٰى}$$

$$\text{وَالنَّبِيُّوْنَ مِنْ رَّبِّهِمْ لَا نُفَرِّقُ بَيْنَ اَحَدٍ مِّنْهُمْ وَنَحْنُ لَهٗ}$$

$$\text{مُسْلِمُوْنَ ﴿٨٤﴾ وَمَنْ يَّبْتَغِ غَيْرَ الْاِسْلٰمِ دِيْنًا فَلَنْ يُّقْبَلَ}$$

$$\text{مِنْهُ وَهُوَ فِى الْاٰخِرَةِ مِنَ الْخٰسِرِيْنَ ﴿٨٥﴾}$$

Do they seek (a religion) other than the Religion of Allah?

Yet to Him has submitted whosoever is in
the heavens and in the earth, willingly or unwillingly,
and to Him shall they (all) be brought back in the end.
Say (O Muslims!): "We believe in Allah and what has been
sent down to us, and that which was sent down to Abraham and
Ishamael and Isaaq and Jacob and their offspring and what was given
to Moses and Jesus and the other Prophets from their Lord.
We make no distinction between any of them, in the matter
of faith and to Allah have we surrendered ourselves."
And whosoever seeks a religion other than Islam,
it shall certainly not be accepted of him;
and in the Hereafter he shall be of the losers.

Al Imran 83,85

Significance: The above *verses* are said to be most effective for the softening of the heart.

AILMENT OF THE HEART

Surah Al-Inshirah

Significance: Recite *Surah Al-Inshirah (30th Juz)* and blow on the patient.

STRENGTHENING THE HEART

The Excellent

Significance: If the above beautiful name of Allah ﷻ is recited a number of times and *blown* on a morsel before eating it, the heart will be strengthened — *Insha Allah*.

TO ACQUIRE FREEDOM FROM MATERIALISM

A.

اَلْوَاحِدُالْأَحَدُ

The One And Only

Significance: To acquire independence in the heart recite the above name of Allah ﷻ 1000 times. The importance of material objects will depart from the reader's heart.

DISEASE OF THE SPLEEN

اِنَّ اللهَ يُمْسِكُ السَّمٰوٰتِ وَالْاَرْضَ اَنْ تَزُوْلَا ۚ

وَلَئِنْ زَالَتَآ اِنْ اَمْسَكَهُمَا مِنْ اَحَدٍ مِّنْ بَعْدِهٖ ؕ اِنَّهٗ

كَانَ حَلِيْمًا غَفُوْرًا ۝

*Lo! Allah grasps the heaven and the earth that they deviate not.
And if they were to deviate there is not one
that could grasp it after that.
Lo! He is For-Ever Clement, Forgiving.*

Fatir 41

Significance: Read the above *ayah* on paper and rub the portion where the spleen is situated. *Insha Allah* the disease will be removed.

FOR A SPECIFIC PAIN

A.

وَبِالْحَقِّ اَنْزَلْنٰهُ وَبِالْحَقِّ نَزَلَ ؕ وَمَآ اَرْسَلْنٰكَ

$$\text{اِلَّا مُبَشِّرًا وَّنَذِيرًا ۞}$$

With truth have we revealed it and with truth
it has descended. And we have not sent you
but as a bearer of good tidings and as a warner.

Bani Israil 105

Significance: Place the hand on the portion where the pain is felt and recite the above *ayah* once and blow thrice on the affected area. *Insha Allah* the pain will disappear.

B.
$$\text{بِسْمِ اللهِ الرَّحْمٰنِ الرَّحِيْمِ ۞}$$

$$\text{اَلْحَمْدُ لِلّٰهِ الَّذِىْ خَلَقَ السَّمٰوٰتِ وَالْاَرْضَ وَجَعَلَ}$$

$$\text{الظُّلُمٰتِ وَالنُّوْرَ ۗ ثُمَّ الَّذِيْنَ كَفَرُوْا بِرَبِّهِمْ يَعْدِلُوْنَ ۞}$$

In the name of Allah, Most Beneficent, Most Merciful.
Praise be to Allah, who has created the heavens and
the earth and has appointed darkness and light.
Yet those who disbelieve ascribe rivals unto their Lord.

Al An'am 1

Significance: A person who recites the above *ayah* 7 times in the morning and 7 times in the evening, then blows on his hands and passes them all over his body, will be safeguarded against all pains and physical calamities.

HEADACHES

A.
$$\text{لَّا يُصَدَّعُوْنَ عَنْهَا وَلَا يُنْزِفُوْنَ ۞}$$

Where from they get no aching of the head nor any madness.

Al Waqiah 19

Significance: Recite the above verse thrice and blow on the patient. The headache will disappear — *Insha Allah*.

B. بِسْمِ اللهِ الرَّحْمٰنِ الرَّحِيْمِ ۞

In the name of Allah, Most Beneficent, Most Merciful

Significance: It is reported that the king of Rome once complained to Umar ؓ about his persistent headache. The Khalifah had a hat (topi) sewn for him. Whenever the king wore it, his headache disappeared. And whenever he took it off, it returned. He became wholly astonished. Curiosity made him open the seams of the headgear, to find the words *"Bismillah"* written beneath the seams.

MIGRAINE

A. Surah Takathur

Significance: Recite Surah Takathur (30th Juz) after Asr Salaah and blow on the head of the patient. This is a very effective remedy for migraine.

B. قُلْ مَنْ رَّبُّ السَّمٰوٰتِ وَالْاَرْضِ ۔ قُلِ اللهُ ۔ قُلْ اَفَاتَّخَذْتُمْ
مِّنْ دُوْنِهٖۤ اَوْلِيَآءَ لَا يَمْلِكُوْنَ لِاَنْفُسِهِمْ نَفْعًا وَّلَا ضَرًّا ۔

Say: Who is the Master of the heavens and earth?

Say: Allah! Say: Yet you take other than Him as friends who possess no power over themselves in giving benefit and difficulty?

Ar Ra'ad 16

Significance: Recite the above *ayah* and blow on the patient. *Insha Allah*, the migraine will disappear.

INFLAMMATION OF THE EYES

A. اَللّٰهُ نُوْرُ السَّمٰوٰتِ وَالْاَرْضِ ۘ مَثَلُ نُوْرِهٖ كَمِشْكٰوةٍ

فِيْهَا مِصْبَاحٌ ۘ اَلْمِصْبَاحُ فِيْ زُجَاجَةٍ ۘ اَلزُّجَاجَةُ كَاَنَّهَا

كَوْكَبٌ دُرِّيٌّ يُّوْقَدُ مِنْ شَجَرَةٍ مُّبٰرَكَةٍ زَيْتُوْنَةٍ لَّا شَرْقِيَّةٍ

وَّلَا غَرْبِيَّةٍ ۙ يَّكَادُ زَيْتُهَا يُضِيْٓءُ وَلَوْ لَمْ تَمْسَسْهُ نَارٌ ۘ نُوْرٌ

عَلٰى نُوْرٍ ۘ يَهْدِى اللّٰهُ لِنُوْرِهٖ مَنْ يَّشَآءُ ۘ وَيَضْرِبُ اللّٰهُ

الْاَمْثَالَ لِلنَّاسِ ۘ وَاللّٰهُ بِكُلِّ شَيْءٍ عَلِيْمٌ ۞ فِيْ بُيُوْتٍ اَذِنَ

اللّٰهُ اَنْ تُرْفَعَ وَيُذْكَرَ فِيْهَا اسْمُهٗ ۙ يُسَبِّحُ لَهٗ فِيْهَا بِالْغُدُوِّ

وَالْاٰصَالِ ۞ رِجَالٌ ۙ لَّا تُلْهِيْهِمْ تِجَارَةٌ وَّلَا بَيْعٌ عَنْ ذِكْرِ اللّٰهِ

وَاِقَامِ الصَّلٰوةِ وَاِيْتَآءِ الزَّكٰوةِ ۙ يَخَافُوْنَ يَوْمًا تَتَقَلَّبُ فِيْهِ

الْقُلُوبُ وَالْاَبْصَرُ ۝ لِيَجْزِيَهُمُ اللّٰهُ اَحْسَنَ مَا عَمِلُوا

وَيَزِيْدَهُمْ مِّنْ فَضْلِهِ ۚ وَاللّٰهُ يَرْزُقُ مَنْ يَّشَاءُ بِغَيْرِ حِسَابٍ ۝

Allah is the Light of the heavens and the earth.
The likeness of His light is as a niche wherein is a lamp,
that lamp is in (a chandelier of) glass, the chandelier is as a
star glittering like a pearl lit from a blessed olive tree,
neither eastern nor western, whose oil is almost luminous
even though no fire touches it.
(This) is all light upon light!
Allah guides unto His light whom
He will. And Allah sets forth all manner of
parables for (the guidance of) mankind.
And verily Allah is Best Knower of all things.
In the houses (of worship) which Allah has ordered to be exalted,
and His name to be remembered therein - extol His Glory
therein in the mornings and the evenings -
By men whom neither trade nor business diverts from the
Remembrance of Allah, and the establishing of prayer
and the paying of the poor-rate (Zakaat).
They keep fearing the Day when hearts will be
unnerved and eyes convulsed (with terror)-
That Allah may recompense them for their best deeds,
and may grant them still more out of His Grace.
And Allah provides for those whom
He will, without measure.

An Nur 35,39

Significance: A person who continually suffers from inflammation of the eyes (conjunctivitis) should recite the above verses thrice daily after Fajr salaah and blow on the back of both thumbs and rub onto both eyes. He will be cured in due course, Insha Allah.

B. Surah Al-Mulk

Significance: *Surah Al-Mulk* should be recited thrice each day for 3 consecutive days. After reciting it 3 times blow on the patient's eyes. The suffering will be alleviated — *Insha Allah*.

STRENGTHENING THE EYESIGHT

A. فَكَشَفْنَا عَنْكَ غِطَآءَكَ فَبَصَرُكَ الْيَوْمَ حَدِيْدٌ ۝

*Now We have removed from you your veil and
this day your sight is iron.*

Qaf 22

Significance: Recite this verse thrice after every *salaah*, blow on the fingers and rub them on the eyes. By doing this the eyesight will never weaken. In fact, any weakness will also disappear.

B. بِسْمِ اللهِ الرَّحْمٰنِ الرَّحِيْمِ ۝

اِنَّآ اَنْزَلْنٰهُ فِيْ لَيْلَةِ الْقَدْرِ ۝ وَمَآ اَدْرٰىكَ

مَا لَيْلَةُ الْقَدْرِ ۝ لَيْلَةُ الْقَدْرِ ۬ خَيْرٌ مِّنْ اَلْفِ شَهْرٍ ۝

تَنَزَّلُ الْمَلٰٓئِكَةُ وَالرُّوْحُ فِيْهَا بِاِذْنِ رَبِّهِمْ ۚ مِّنْ كُلِّ اَمْرٍ ۝

سَلٰمٌ ۡ هِيَ حَتّٰى مَطْلَعِ الْفَجْرِ ۝

No doubt, We sent down this blessed Qur'an in Night of Power.

59

And what will explain to you know what the Night of Power if?
The Night of Power is better than a thousand months.
The angels and the (Holy) Spirit (Gabriel) descend in it by the
Command of their Lord for every affair (of good).
It is all (peace and) security till the rise of the dawn.

Al Qadr 1,5

Significance: Anyone who gazes towards the sky while in the state of *Wudhu* and reads the above *Surah*, his eyesight will never weaken — *Insha Allah*.

PAIN IN THE KIDNEY

Significance: Recite *Surah Quraish* (30th Juz) and blow on any food before consuming it. The pain will disappear — *Insha Allah*.

EPILEPSY

بِسْــــمِ اللهِ الرَّحْمٰنِ الرَّحِيَمِ الٓمٓصٓ طٰسٓمٓ كٓهٰيٰعٓصٓ .A

يٰسَ وَالْقُرْاٰنِ الْحَكِيْمِ حٰمٓ عٓسٓقٓ نٓ وَالْقَلَمِ وَمَا يَسْطُرُوْنَ

Significance: It is reported of a certain sage that his domestic servant had continuous bouts of epileptic fits. On one such occasion he recited the above words of the *Holy Qur'an* in her ears. She immediately came to and never had the attack all her life.

B. Surah Ash-Shams

Significance: Reciting Surah Ash-Shams (30th Juz) in the patient's ear is believed to be very beneficial for epilepsy.

PARALYSIS OF THE BODY

A. هُوَ اللّٰهُ الَّذِىْ لَاۤ اِلٰهَ اِلَّا هُوَ ۚ عٰلِمُ الْغَيْبِ وَالشَّهٰدَةِ ۚ

هُوَ الرَّحْمٰنُ الرَّحِيْمُ ۩ هُوَ اللّٰهُ الَّذِىْ لَاۤ اِلٰهَ اِلَّا هُوَ ۚ

اَلْمَلِكُ الْقُدُّوْسُ السَّلٰمُ الْمُؤْمِنُ الْمُهَيْمِنُ الْعَزِيْزُ الْجَبَّارُ

الْمُتَكَبِّرُ ۚ سُبْحٰنَ اللّٰهِ عَمَّا يُشْرِكُوْنَ ۩ هُوَ اللّٰهُ

الْخَالِقُ الْبَارِئُ الْمُصَوِّرُ لَهُ الْاَسْمَآءُ الْحُسْنٰى ۚ يُسَبِّحُ لَهٗ

مَا فِى السَّمٰوٰتِ وَالْاَرْضِ ۚ وَهُوَ الْعَزِيْزُ الْحَكِيْمُ ۩

وَنُنَزِّلُ مِنَ الْقُرْاٰنِ مَا هُوَ شِفَآءٌ وَّرَحْمَةٌ لِّلْمُؤْمِنِيْنَ

وَلَا يَزِيْدُ الظّٰلِمِيْنَ اِلَّا خَسَارًا ۩

He is Allah, besides Whom there is none to be worshipped;
Knower of everything hidden and open.
He it is the Most-Kind, the Ever-Merciful.
He is Allah-besides Whom there is none to be worshipped;
the Sovereign of all, the Most Holy, the Bestower of Peace,
the Giver of Security, the Guardian over all, the Esteemed One,
the Mender of broken hearts, the Exalted in Might.
Glory be to Allah from what they associate with Him.
He is Allah, the Creator of all, the Maker of all,

the Fashioner of all, His are all most beautiful names,
Whatever is in the heavens and the earth glorifies Him;
and He it is - the All-Powerful, the All-Wise.
And We send down in the Qur'an that which is a (means of)
healing and a mercy to the Believers from end to end,
and the Qur'an only increases the wrongdoers in loss.

Significance: Ibnu Qutaibah R.A. reports that he once inquired from a person who was completely cured from paralysis, the secret to his cure. He replied that he had blown on *Zam Zam* water and drank it. He was completely cured of his paralysis.

LEPROSY

A. وَاَيُّوْبَ اِذْ نَادٰى رَبَّهٗٓ اَنِّيْ مَسَّنِيَ الضُّرُّ

وَاَنْتَ اَرْحَمُ الرّٰحِمِيْنَ ۞

And remember Ayyoob when he cried to His Lord:
"Truly distress has seized me, but You are the Most Merciful
of those who are Merciful.

Al Ambiya 83

Significance: Ibnu Qutaibah ﷺ reports that a certain leper whose flesh was about to disintegrate, consulted a sage for a cure. The latter recited the relevant verse and blew on him. This caused new skin to appear on his body and he was completely cured. The verse recited by the sage is the above *ayah*.

B. اَلْمَجِيْدُ

Most Venerable

Significance: If a leper fasts on the 13th, 14th and 15th of any lunar month and recites the above attribute of Allah ﷻ excessively each day at the time of breaking his fast, he will be cured of the disease — *Insha Allah.*

C.

بِسْمِ اللهِ الرَّحْمٰنِ الرَّحِيْمِ ۩

اَنِّيْ قَدْ جِئْتُكُمْ بِاٰيَةٍ مِّنْ رَّبِّكُمْ ۙ اَنِّيْ اَخْلُقُ لَكُمْ

مِّنَ الطِّيْنِ كَهَيْئَةِ الطَّيْرِ فَاَنْفُخُ فِيْهِ فَيَكُوْنُ طَيْرًا بِاِذْنِ اللهِ ۚ

وَاُبْرِئُ الْاَكْمَهَ وَالْاَبْرَصَ وَاُحْيِ الْمَوْتٰى بِاِذْنِ اللهِ ۚ

وَاُنَبِّئُكُمْ بِمَا تَأْكُلُوْنَ وَمَا تَدَّخِرُوْنَ ۙ فِيْ بُيُوْتِكُمْ ۚ اِنَّ فِيْ ذٰلِكَ

لَاٰيَةً لَّكُمْ اِنْ كُنْتُمْ مُّؤْمِنِيْنَ ۩

In the name of Allah, Most Beneficent, Most Merciful
'Surely I have come to you with a Sign (miracle) from your Lord:
surely I make for you out of clay the form of a bird,
then I breathe into this lifeless form and
it becomes a living bird by the will of Allah;
and I heal the born blind and cure the incurable leper,
and bring the dead to life by the will of Allah;
and I declare to you what you eat and
what you keep stored in your houses -
surely there is a great Sign for you of my truth
in these miracles, if you are true believers.

Al Imr`an 49

Significance: It is reported from Kalbi that a certain person who was afflicted with leprosy related to him that the disease had taken its toll on him to such an extent that he found it embarrassing to sit near anyone owing to the offensive smell his body gave off. However, one day he met a pious person and complained to him about his illness. The sage recited a verse from the *Qur'an* over water and made him drink it. In a few days he was cured. The verse recited by the sage is the above *ayah*.

ITCHING OF THE BODY

فَكَسَوْنَا الْعِظَمَ لَحْمًا ۵ ثُمَّ اَنْشَاْنٰهُ خَلْقًا اٰخَرَ ط

فَتَبَارَكَ اللّٰهُ اَحْسَنُ الْخٰلِقِيْنَ ﴿١٤﴾

And We clothed the bones with flesh;
then We made it into another creature.
Thus exalted is Allah, The Best of Creators.

Al Mu'minun 14

Significance: It is reported that a certain person's body itched a great deal owing to some type of rash he suffered from. For a long time he tried all remedies, but to no avail. Finally, one day he decided to join a caravan heading for *Makkah*. By the time the caravan reached the tomb of Ali ﷺ this person became so tired that he decided to remain at the tomb. The caravan left without him. That night he saw and heard Ali ﷺ in his dream recite the above verses.

When he awoke in the morning there was not the slightest trace of the sickness.

BONE FRACTURE

$$\text{فَاِنْ تَوَلَّوْا فَقُلْ حَسْبِيَ اللهُ لَآ اِلٰهَ اِلَّا هُوَ عَلَيْهِ تَوَكَّلْتُ}$$

$$\text{وَهُوَ رَبُّ الْعَرْشِ الْعَظِيْمِ ﴿١٢٩﴾}$$

But if they turn away, say: 'Allah suffices me:
There is none worthy of worship but He: upon Him is my trust —
He is Lord of the Great Throne.'

At Tawbah 129

Significance: Laith bin Sa'ad R.A. reports that a certain person sustained an injury as a result of which his thigh-bone broke. A man appeared in his dream. He placed his hand on the affected area and recited the above *verse*. His thigh healed in a short period of time.

The above *verse* is also said to be very effective in affording its reader safety against falling from a high place, drowning and being struck by iron. Abud-Darda is reported as saying that a person who recites it 100 times daily, all his worldly needs and needs pertaining to the hereafter will be fulfilled.

FORGETFULNESS

$$\text{اَلرَّحْمٰنُ}$$

The Compassionate

Significance: Read the above Beautiful Name of Allah ﷻ 100 times after every salaah. Forgetfulness, negligence and stupor will be warded off — Insha Allah.

TO REMOVE HARDHEARTEDNESS

The Most Merciful

Significance: Recite the above attribute of Allah ﷻ 100 times everyday. Hardheartedness will be replaced with affection, tenderness, kindness and compassion — *Insha Allah*.

BARAKAH IN FOOD

Significance: A'ishah ◉ reports that a person came to Rasulullah ﷺ and complained that there was no barakah blessings in his home. Rasulullah ﷺ asked: *"Why are you negligent of Ayatul Kursi? Whoever reads it upon any food, Allah ﷻ will impart barakah to such food."*

THE PRICE OF JANNAH

Significance: Abu Umamah Sa'd ibn Ajalaan ◉ says that Rasulullah ﷺ said that anyone who recites *Ayatul Kursi* after Fardh *salaah,* the only thing that prevents him from going to *Jannah* is death.

NIGHTMARES

لَهُمُ الْبُشْرٰى فِى الْحَيٰوةِ الدُّنْيَا وَفِى الْاٰخِرَةِ ط لَا تَبْدِيْلَ لِكَلِمٰتِ اللهِ ط ذٰلِكَ هُوَ الْفَوْزُ الْعَظِيْمُ ۞

For them are glad tidings in the life of this
world and the hereafter.
There is no change in the word of Allah.
This is, without doubt, supreme felicity.

Yunus 64

Significance: The above could be recited before sleeping by one who has continuous nightmares.

INSOMNIA

Surely, Allah and His angels send salawaat
(blessings) on the Nabi. O you who believe,
(you too) send salawaat and salutations on him.

Al Ahzab 56

Significance: To beat insomnia and have a good night's sleep read the above verse excessively.

THE 99 BEAUTIFUL NAMES OF ALLAH ﷻ

Significance: Memorising and reading the 99 Beautiful Names of Allah ﷻ is an act of great merit. Glad-tidings of admittance into *Jannah* is given. Any *du'a* made after its recitation is assuredly accepted. Reciting it after Fajr *salaah* entails the assured acceptance of *du'a* and the attraction of Allah's mercy. The method of reciting is to say *Jalla Jallaluhu* after each attribute of Allah ﷻ.

FOR PROTECTION AGAINST THIEVES

٨. اٰمَنَ الرَّسُوْلُ بِمَآ اُنْزِلَ اِلَيْهِ مِنْ رَّبِّهٖ وَالْمُؤْمِنُوْنَ ۚ

كُلٌّ اٰمَنَ بِاللهِ وَمَلٰٓئِكَتِهٖ وَكُتُبِهٖ وَرُسُلِهٖ ۚ لَا نُفَرِّقُ بَيْنَ

اَحَدٍ مِّنْ رُّسُلِهٖ ۚ وَقَالُوْا سَمِعْنَا وَاَطَعْنَا غُفْرَانَكَ رَبَّنَا

وَاِلَيْكَ الْمَصِيْرُ ﴿٢٨٥﴾ لَا يُكَلِّفُ اللهُ نَفْسًا اِلَّا وُسْعَهَا ۚ

لَهَا مَا كَسَبَتْ وَعَلَيْهَا مَا اكْتَسَبَتْ ۚ رَبَّنَا لَا تُؤَاخِذْنَآ

اِنْ نَّسِيْنَآ اَوْ اَخْطَأْنَا ۚ رَبَّنَا وَلَا تَحْمِلْ عَلَيْنَآ اِصْرًا

كَمَا حَمَلْتَهٗ عَلَى الَّذِيْنَ مِنْ قَبْلِنَا ۚ رَبَّنَا وَلَا تُحَمِّلْنَا

مَا لَا طَاقَةَ لَنَا بِهٖ ۚ وَاعْفُ عَنَّا ۗ وَاغْفِرْ لَنَا ۗ وَارْحَمْنَا ۗ

اَنْتَ مَوْلٰىنَا فَانْصُرْنَا عَلَى الْقَوْمِ الْكٰفِرِيْنَ ﴿٢٨٦﴾

*The (Holy) Apostle believes in that (Book) which has been
sent down to him from his Lord; and so do the believers.
Each one believes in all sincerity in Allah and His Angels and His
Books and His Apostles; (and they proclaim):*

"We discriminate not against any of His Apostles."
And they say: "We hear, and we obey.
We seek Your Forgiveness, O our Lord, and it is
You to Whom we all are to return in the end."
Allah does not burden any soul with more than it can bear.
For it hall be the reward of what (good) it has earned,
and against it shall be (the punishment of)
what (evil) it has committed:
"Our Lord! call us not to account if we forget or err.
Our Lord! lay not on us such a (heavy) burden as
You did lay on those who have passed away before us.
Our Lord! lay not on us that burden
which we have not the strength to bear.
And pardon us; absolve us; and have mercy on us;
You alone are our Friend and Helper;
help us to triumph over the unbelieving folk."

Al Baqarah 285,286

Significance: Anyone who recites the above verses before going to bed, his wealth, property and life will be safeguarded against all calamities.

B. AYATUL-KURSI

Significance: A person who recites *Ayatul-Kursi* after every *salaah*, and in the morning and evening, and on entering the house, and when going to bed, he will becomes self-sufficient; Allah will grant him sustenance from unimaginable sources; belongings and property will be protected from burglaries; his sustenance (*rizq*) will increase; and he will never be afflicted with poverty. And wherever it is recited, burglars would not dare to visit that place.

C.   فَاِذَا اسْتَوَيْتَ اَنْتَ وَمَنْ مَّعَكَ عَلَى الْفُلْكِ فَقُلِ

الْحَمْدُ لِلَّهِ الَّذِىْ نَجَّانَا مِنَ الْقَوْمِ الظَّلِمِيْنَ ۝ وَقُلْ

رَبِّ اَنْزِلْنِيْ مُنْزَلاً مُّبَارَكًا وَّاَنْتَ خَيْرُ الْمُنْزِلِيْنَ ۝

And when you have embarked on the ark —
you and those with you — say:
"Praise be to Allah who has saved us from
the people who do wrong".
And say: "O my Lord, enable me to disembark with (Your)
blessings for you are the best to enable us to disembark".
Al Mu'minun 28,29

Significance: Recitation of the above affords the reciter and his family protection against thieves, enemies and Jinn.

SAFEGUARDING OF MONEY AND VALUABLES

Significance: For safekeeping of money, recite *Surah Al-Asr* (30th Juz) when banking it or putting it in a safe place or hiding it anywhere. The same applies to valuables.

TO FIND A LOST OBJECT

A.

إِنَّا لِلَّهِ وَإِنَّا إِلَيْهِ رَجِعُوْنَ ۝

We belong to Allah and to Him shall we return.
Al Baqarah 156

Significance: Recite the above *ayah* and search for the lost object. Insha Allah it will be found. Otherwise, something better and greater in value will be received.

B. Surah Adh-Dhuha

Significance: Recite Surah Adh-Dhuha (30th Juz) seven times. The lost item will be found — *Insha Allah*.

C.

And He found you distracted in His love,
so He led you on the way to guidance.

Ad Duha 7

Significance: Recite *Surah Adh-Duha* (30th Juz) once. But repeat the above verse thrice. The lost item will be found — *Insha Allah*.

FOR THE RETURN OF SOMEONE WHO HAS ABSCONDED

Suratud-Duhaa

Significance: Recite *Suratud-Duhaa* seven times. *Insha Allah,* the runaway will return.

ENSURING THE SAFETY OF ONE'S FAMILY AND PROPERTY DURING ONE'S ABSENCE

The Guardian

Significance: Before undertaking a journey, recite the above attribute of Allah ﷻ seven times:

Doing this, there will be no need to worry about their safety until one returns.

PROTECTION AGAINST ALL TYPES OF ANIMALS, INSECTS AND REPTILES

وَكَلْبُهُمْ بٰسِطٌ ذِرَاعَيْهِ بِالْوَصِيْدِ ط

*And their dog stretching forth his
two fore-legs on the threshold.*

Al Khaf 18

Significance: When a dog poses a threat — The following verse should be recited when a dog growls or is about to attack. The same applies to any other wild animal such as a lion, cheetah etc. The above *verse*.

PROTECTION AGAINST SNAKES AND SCORPIONS

اِنَّ رَبَّكُمُ اللّٰهُ الَّذِىْ خَلَقَ السَّمٰوٰتِ وَالْاَرْضَ فِى سِتَّةِ

اَيَّامٍ ثُمَّ اسْتَوٰى عَلَى الْعَرْشِ يُغْشِى الَّيْلَ النَّهَارَ يَطْلُبُهٗ

حَثِيْثًا لا وَّالشَّمْسَ وَالْقَمَرَ وَالنُّجُوْمَ مُسَخَّرٰتٍ بِاَمْرِهٖ ط

اَلَا لَهُ الْخَلْقُ وَالْاَمْرُ ط تَبَارَكَ اللّٰهُ رَبُّ الْعٰلَمِيْنَ ۞

اُدْعُوْا رَبَّكُمْ تَضَرُّعًا وَّخُفْيَةً ط اِنَّهٗ لَا يُحِبُّ الْمُعْتَدِيْنَ ۞

وَلَا تُفْسِدُوْا فِى الْاَرْضِ بَعْدَ اِصْلٰحِهَا وَادْعُوْهُ

خَوْفًا وَّطَمَعًا ۪اِنَّ رَحْمَتَ اللّٰهِ قَرِيْبٌ مِّنَ الْمُحْسِنِيْنَ ۝

Surely your Lord is Allah, Who created the heavens and
the earth in Six Days, then established Himself on the
Throne (of high Authority) befitting His Supreme Majesty.
He covers the night and the day by each other following swiftly;
and (He created) the sun and the moon and the stars,
all subservient to His Command. Listen!
His is the Creation and His is the Command.
Blessed is Allah, the Lord and Cherisher of all the Worlds!
Call on your Lord in all humility and in secrecy and
surely Allah loves not these who trespass limits.
And do not make mischief in the earth after it has been set
right and call on Him fearing and hoping (in your heart of hearts).
Surely the Mercy of Allah is nigh to the doers of good.

Al A'raf 54,56

Significance: With the recital of the above verses, snakes and scorpions will not be able to harm — *Insha Allah*.

TO PREVENT DANGEROUS ANIMALS, HARMFUL INSECTS AND REPTILES FROM ENTERING THE HOUSE

A. اِنِّىْ تَوَكَّلْتُ عَلَى اللّٰهِ رَبِّىْ وَرَبِّكُمْ ۪مَا مِنْ دَآبَّةٍ اِلَّا هُوَ

اٰخِذٌۢ بِنَاصِيَتِهَا اِنَّ رَبِّىْ عَلٰى صِرَاطٍ مُّسْتَقِيْمٍ ۝

Indeed, I rely in Allah, my Lord and your Lord.
There is no animal but He grasps it by its forelock.
Surely, my Lord is on the Straight Path.

Al Hud 56

Significance: Recite the above verse excessively — especially when going to bed and on awakening.

WHEN FEARING AN ATTACK FROM AN ANIMAL

A. اَللهُ رَبُّنَا وَرَبُّكُمْ ﺀ لَنَآ اَعْمٰلُنَا وَلَكُمْ اَعْمٰلُكُمْ ﺀ

لَا حُجَّةَ بَيْنَنَا وَبَيْنَكُمْ ﺀ اَللهُ يَجْمَعُ بَيْنَنَا ﺀ

Allah is our Lord and your Lord.
For us is our deeds and for you, yours.
There is no argument between us and you.
Allah will bring us together.

Ash Shura 15

Significance: Read the above *ayah* and blow towards the animal. It won't attack — *Insha Allah.*

WHEN BITTEN BY A POISONOUS INSECT OR SNAKE

And when you grasp, you grasp like
men with absolute power.

Ash Shu'ara 130

Significance: Circulate the finger around the bitten area and recite the above verse seven times in one breath. The patient will recover shortly — Insha Allah.

WHEN STUNG BY AN INSECT

Significance: Recite *Suratul Inshirah* (30th Juz) and blow on the patient. The pain will subside shortly – *Insha Allah*.

GENERAL PROTECTION

اَلْحَفِيْظُ

The Protector

Significance: Recite the above name of Allah excessively. No harm will be caused to the reciter even if he sleeps in a place where wild animals abound.

TO DRIVE OUT ANTS FROM THE HOUSE

يَاأَيُّهَا النَّمْلُ ادْخُلُوا مَسَاكِنَكُمْ لَا يَحْطِمَنَّكُمْ سُلَيْمٰنُ
وَجُنُودُهُ وَهُمْ لَا يَشْعُرُونَ ۝

O ants, enter your dwellings (so) Sulaimaan and his army do not trample you without knowing it.

An Naml 18

Significance: Upon reciting this verse, they will disappear very shortly – *Insha Allah*.

TO DRIVE OUT MOSQUITOES, FLEAS, ETC

وَمَا لَنَا اَلَّا نَتَوَكَّلَ عَلَى اللهِ وَقَدْ هَدٰنَا سُبُلَنَا وَلَنَصْبِرَنَّ

عَلَىٰ مَآ اٰذَيْتُمُوْنَا ۚ وَعَلَى اللّٰهِ فَلْيَتَوَكَّلِ الْمُتَوَكِّلُوْنَ ﴿١٢﴾

How should we not put our trust in Allah
when He has shown us our ways.
We will surely endure that hurt which you cause us.
And in Allah let the trusting put their trust.

Ibrahim 12

Significance: To drive out mosquitoes, fleas etc. from the house or bedroom recite the above verse numerous times, the night will pass without disturbance — *Insha Allah.*

RELEASE FROM IMPRISONMENT

رَبَّنَآ اَخْرِجْنَا مِنْ هٰذِهِ الْقَرْيَةِ الظَّالِمِ اَهْلُهَا ۚ وَّاجْعَلْ

لَّنَا مِنْ لَّدُنْكَ وَلِيًّا ۙ وَّاجْعَلْ لَّنَا مِن لَّدُنْكَ نَصِيْرًا ﴿٧٥﴾

Our Lord, take us out of this town whose people are oppressors
and raise for us from yourself one who will protect us
and raise for us from yourself one who will help us.

An Nisa 75

Significance: If a person is trapped in a country or town as a result of the country or town being under siege or due to any other reason such as curfew etc. he should recite the above verse excessively. He will soon find a way out — *Insha Allah.*

A MUSLIM'S INVISIBLE ENEMIES AND THE WAY TO OVERCOME THEM:

Allah explained to Muslims that they have hidden enemies, who do their best to mislead Muslims to disrespect Allah in this worldly life and to his displeasure in the Hereafter. Allah also guided Muslims to the method of delivery from the evils of these unseen enemies. The first of these enemies is the accursed Satan, who stirs up and leads all other enemies of man. Satan was not only a foe to our forefather Adam and our great grandmother Eve, but he is an open enemy of Adam's progeny till the end of this wordly life. Satan strives hard to persuade people either to disbelief or to commit sins in order that they may accompany him in dwelling forever in Hell. Satan is an incorporeal spirit, able to instill evil in man and allure mischief to him as if it were a second nature to him.

Allah explained to us how to overcome Satan and his followers. When a Muslim is about to commit a sin, or when he is maddened with anger, he should say:

$$\text{اَعُوْذُ بِاللهِ مِنَ الشَّيْطٰنِ الرَّجِيْمِ}$$

"I ask Allah for His refuge against the accursed Satan."

Then he should refrain himself from committing the sin and calm his anger. The Muslim should know that malicious incentives are always motivated by the Satan.

Allah said:

$$\text{اِنَّ الشَّيْطٰنَ لَكُمْ عَدُوٌّ فَاتَّخِذُوْهُ عَدُوًّا ۤ اِنَّمَا يَدْعُوْا}$$

$$\text{حِزْبَهٗ لِيَكُوْنُوْا مِنْ اَصْحٰبِ السَّعِيْرِ ۝}$$

"Surely, Satan is an enemy to you, so treat him as an enemy.

اللَّهُمَّ إِنِّي أَسْأَلُكَ يَا اللَّهُ بِأَنَّكَ الْوَاحِدُ الْأَحَدُ الصَّمَدُ الَّذِي لَمْ يَلِدْ وَلَمْ يُولَدْ وَلَمْ يَكُنْ لَهُ كُفُواً أَحَدٌ، أَنْ تَغْفِرَ لِي ذُنُوبِي إِنَّكَ أَنْتَ الْغَفُورُ الرَّحِيمُ

Allāhumma innee as-aluka yā Allāhu bi annakal wāhidul ahadus-samad allaḏhi lam yalid wa lam yūlad wa lam yakul-lahū kufuwan-ahad. antaghfira li ḏhunūbi innaka antal-ghafūrur-rahim

> O Allah, I ask You. O Allah, You are the One, the Only, Self-Sufficient Master, Who was not begotten and begets not and none is equal to Him. Forgive me my sins, surely you are Forgiving, Merciful.

اللَّهُمَّ إِنِّي ظَلَمْتُ نَفْسِي ظُلْماً كَثِيراً، وَلَا يَغْفِرُ الذُّنُوبَ إِلَّا أَنْتَ، فَاغْفِرْ لِي مَغْفِرَةً مِنْ عِنْدِكَ وَارْحَمْنِي إِنَّكَ أَنْتَ الْغَفُورُ الرَّحِيمُ

Allāhumma innee ḏhalamtu nafsi ḏhulman katheerā wa lā yaghfiruḏh- ḏhunūba illa anta, faghfirli maghfiratan min 'indika warhamni innaka antal ghafūrur-rahim

> O Allah, I have greatly wronged myself and no one forgives sins but You. So grant me forgiveness, forgiveness from You, and have mercy on me. Surely, You are Forgiving, Merciful. [Bukhari & Muslim]

رَبَّنَا لَا تُزِغْ قُلُوبَنَا بَعْدَ إِذْ هَدَيْتَنَا وَهَبْ لَنَا مِن لَّدُنكَ رَحْمَةً إِنَّكَ أَنتَ الْوَهَّابُ

Rabbanā lā tuzigh quloobanā ba'da idh hadaitanā wa hab lanā milladunka rahmah innaka antal-Wahhāb

> (Who say), "Our Lord, let not our hearts deviate after You have guided us and grant us from Yourself mercy. Indeed, You are the Bestower." [3:6]

Made in the USA
Monee, IL
21 February 2025

12702206R00046